Whitetail Wisdom

Whitetail Wisdom

Hunter's Information Series®
North American Hunting Club
Minneapolis, Minnesota

Whitetail Wisdom

Copyright © 1997, North American Hunting Club

All rights reserved.

ISBN 0-914697-73-0

Printed in U.S.A.

2   3   4   5   6   7   8   9   10

Acknowledgements

Compiled & Edited by the staff of North American Hunter magazine:

Bill Miller – Editor
Gregg Gutschow – Managing Editor
Mike Faw – Associate Editor
Debra Morem – Senior Editorial Assistant

Mike Vail – Executive In Charge
Steve Perlstein – Production Manager

Contents

North American Hunting Club Executive Director Bill Miller (left) on a more recent hunt with Larry Weishuhn. This time they're grinning over one of Larry's bucks!

Introduction

*L*arry Weishuhn still kids me about it. It was our first hunt together. We were on an incredible ranch in the Texas Hill Country. In the first two days we had seen numbers of 10-, 12-, and yes, even 14-point bucks. These deer were feeding calmly within easy range of my scoped Thompson/Center Contender .30-30 Win. pistol. Yet I hadn't squeezed the trigger once, not even cocked the hammer.

The problem was that I only had permission to shoot a mature 8-point buck or what's known in Texas as a cull buck or management deer. These are deer which have grown old without developing trophy caliber antlers and need to be removed from the gene pool. As far as I could tell, this ranch didn't have any such deer. After two days, Larry was starting to agree with me.

I was worried because I only had one day left to hunt, so that evening we tracked down the ranch manager and laid out our problem to him. With typical Texas hospitality he said, "Well, I guess if all our old 8-points are gone, you'll have to find an old 10-point." Though I managed to maintain control to shake his hand, I was leaping in the air, clicking my heels and "yee-hawing" on the inside.

The next day Larry and I set up over a feeding area in a deluxe Texas-style shooting house. This thing was bigger than the "club house" my brother and I shared when we were kids. It easily accommodated both Larry and I, though I cast a fairly large shadow and Larry's is longer than mine!

Anyway we watched many bucks drift in and out, checking the does which would soon be ready for breeding. One particular 10-point came early and stayed late. He was an old buck who moved with a distinctly arthritic gate. His rack would score 150 to 155 B&C points.

Over the afternoon, Larry and I talked calmly about the buck, comparing his rack to other deer that showed up and left. He stayed. Finally, as the afternoon sky began to think about getting dark, Larry said, "Well, I guess you'd better shoot him so we can take some pictures before dark."

One moment, I was calm, cool and collected readily discussing antler growth, stickers, kickers and ginger bread. The next I was a quivering wreck. Despite resting the forearm of the Contender on a sandbag in the window of the shooting house, I couldn't keep the 2X scope anywhere close to on the shoulder of the buck just 60 yards away! Major league buck fever had set in!

Larry whispered me through it, and in a couple of minutes I was again composed and ready to shoot. When the pistol bucked, the deer dropped.

In a quarter century of hunting, I don't recollect ever going from calculating hunter to total basket case quite that fast. Sure since then I've cried when I've taken game with my dad's old guns, and I've trembled when I've held one of my dogs' first retrieves, and I've choked up walking up on fallen deer. But most times, these days, the fever sets in after the game is down.

That is until the *North American Hunter* team sat down to plan the book you're reading right now. I honest to gosh felt "the fever" when I thought of the great book we could provide NAHC members if we searched the pages of the magazines all the way back to the Club's earliest days.

More than any other project we've ever worked on at the North American Hunting Club I really believe <u>Whitetail Wisdom</u> can be called "the best of the best from the best."

The magazine staff searched through nearly two decades of back issues to assemble a list of every white-tailed deer hunting feature ever to appear in the pages of *North American Hunter*. Then we considered each one, arguing its merits and its shortcomings and recollecting what NAHC members commented on the story when it ran. Our measuring tape was whether the tips, tactics and strategies presented in the story still apply and whether they've proven true over the years. Our goal was to present North American Hunting

Club members with a book that will stand out head and shoulders above the rest as the most informative and useful deer hunting book ever assembled.

We believe we've achieved that...and more! For new members of the NAHC, this book will provide access to those years of incredibly valuable hunting lore they missed when they weren't members. For longtime and Life Members, <u>Whitetail Wisdom</u> will provide a convenient, easy to read index of all those deer hunting stories you dig back through the old magazines to find.

Researching this project was easy. The tough part was selecting which pieces should appear because there is so much good material from so many good hunters and writers.

Many of the frequent contributors to *North American Hunter* magazine have become my best friends. They are hunters and writers who are indeed legendary figures. By the grace of God, I've been fortunate enough to share campfires, horseback rides, shooting benches and sunrises with many of them. I can tell you, first hand, the authors whose work appears in <u>Whitetail Wisdom</u> know deer and deer hunting. That's how their stories got into the pages of *North American Hunter* to begin with, and it's how they made the cut for this book.

The roster of contributors to <u>Whitetail Wisdom</u> reads like a "Who's Who" list of the deer hunting world. Larry Weishuhn, J. Wayne Fears, Jim Shockey, Nick Sisley, Chuck Adams, Gary Clancy, Grant Wood, Charles Alsheimer, Richard Smith, Greg Miller, Jeff Murray, C.J. Winand, John Phillips...and the list goes on.

Personally, I'm a much better deer hunter today than when I started with the NAHC those many years ago. Sure, a good bit of it is from more years and more hours each year in the woods. Yet at least an equal contributor is from reading the stories in this book and talking with the hunters who wrote them.

I hope that after reading <u>Whitetail Wisdom</u> you feel the same way and that the book becomes a treasured addition to your hunting library.

Take care and good hunting,

Bill Miller
Executive Director

Understanding
Trophy Bucks

Do Big Bucks Really Think?

by Bob Grewell

Whitetail movement interrupted the serenity of the late November morning. A fat 8-point buck appeared from the distant woods, crossing the 50-acre, knee-high weed and stubble field at a leisurely pace. I watched him from my secure tree stand until he leaped over a dried-up drainage ditch and was lost from view on a briar-infested hillside.

This was the third morning in a row I had studied this creek-bottom crossing. Two of the last three mornings, the buck traveled the field in a diagonal manner, using the pre-dawn's low light to help disguise his movements.

As soon as he was out of sight, and had been for some time, I decided to take the time to scout his habitat to see if I could better understand his movements.

I spent the remaining hours of the morning backtracking his trail, ending at a massive field of standing corn encircled by a shielding strip of waist-high weeds. This quadrant of ideal white-tailed deer habitat was located on the opposite side of a narrow stream.

After finding this choice spot, I was more confident I had a good, or at least a better, idea of his general pattern of travel. On one of the next few mornings I would intercept him at his usual stream crossing and take him just as his hooves touched the opposite dirt bank. I was sure my plan was foolproof.

Three mornings later, I still hadn't tagged him. So, on the fourth morning, I positioned myself in my original location. Sure enough, well before good light he crossed the open weed field in his usual manner.

Understandably, I didn't want to get too close to his bedding location. Besides, there were no appropriate trees close at the edges of the weed field where I could set up an elevated ambush.

I decided to get down on the ground and try to take him.

I was completely camouflaged, scent cautious and as quiet and motionless as humanly possible. I played the wind in my favor.

Three more mornings went by and still no buck. So I went back to the tree from where I originally spotted him. Sure enough! I spotted him again!

The next three days, the evasive buck made no appearance while I was hunting. On the fourth morning, he popped into view, only this time the buck was using another trail on the opposite side of the field. His intended destination appeared to be the same, but he approached it from a different direction.

Try I as I did, I could find no pattern to this buck's behavior. He seemingly would change his route of travel on a whim. It was almost enough to make a hunter believe this buck was consciously avoiding his pursuer by planning his movements.

The white-tailed buck is a magnificent animal that gains ever more respect from the hunter who pursues him on a one-on-one basis. White-tailed bucks can make you curse, lose sleep, spend more money than your budget will really allow, and cause you to hurry from one place to another as you attempt to ambush him.

Hunting a "thinking" buck is a unique experience because each deer we face will expose characteristics about itself that you can use to your advantage in pursuit of the individual deer. That's what makes hunting a white-tailed buck exciting each time you enter his habitat. You can't be sure how any given deer will react. And sometimes it seems, as in the case of the farm-country buck I was after, you can't be sure how a buck you think you know is going to act.

Sometimes you'll run across a buck that turns out to be fairly easy to take, but those are rare exceptions that prove the rule. Others, well...they can make you pull out your hair.

Whitetails, especially seasoned bucks that have been educated by hunting pressure, appear to be capable of thinking, making decisions, planning their intentions or controlling each situation in their favor. The more time a hunter spends with deer in their natural habitat, the more he or she will begin to believe that wild animals, especially bucks that have been badgered by human hunters, have a certain degree of "personality."

I am in no way suggesting that deer are really thinking, reasoning, mentally capable creatures that can compete with humans by using the same type of intellect as we possess. But it's obvious that "hunter cautious" bucks have a type of personality that instructs them to act and react differently under various situations.

Whitetail personality might be established by the numerous kinds of past experiences they have faced, sudden changes in their environment, or how much and what types of hunting pressure they have experienced. Any or all of these circumstances can have a direct influence on the way a buck reacts, whether negative or positive. One deer will react one way to a given stimuli, and the next day the same deer might do just the opposite.

Not long ago, an avid hunting friend of mine was concentrating on a specific eye-opening, unpressured 10-point buck that was methodic about using the same tree-lined fence row. This natural landscape structure connected a rolling cornfield with a creek bottom crossing that led to a discouragingly dense bedding thicket.

The initial stand setup this hunter established was erected during the first week of legal hunting season. The second day afield, he was able to get off a clean shot. Unfortunately, his arrow glided high over the buck's left shoulder.

The buck bolted and ran some 80 yards away before stopping to look back in the direction of the hunter's concealed tree stand site on the fence line. The buck stared for a few seconds, then loped off toward an adjacent wood. Because the buck had been alarmed, the hunter chose to let the hunting area rest for a week and pursue deer elsewhere.

With no luck at two other hunting spots, this same hunter went back to his original tree line a week later, anxious to hunt the 10-pointer again. The first morning, just after the sun fanned its rays over the edge of the horizon, he noticed the buck casually leaving the standing corn, making its way along the fence row, headed directly toward his stand.

When the buck was about 50 yards away, it veered away from the fence line and swung out into the open field before continuing along the fence line. The buck stopped once and looked directly toward the hunter's stand site. Then it proceeded through the weed field well out of range of the hunter's arrow.

After it was almost 100 yards from the hunter, the buck moved back over closer to the fence line before disappearing over a small rise.

The buck avoided the hunter as if it had planned the action. The best chance this hunter had now was to change locations and set up on the buck at a different spot.

What had caused the buck to shy away from the hunter's location? The hunter was perfectly camouflaged, the wind was in his favor, and he was well-concealed. The buck had a week to forget about the alarming encounter. So, it seemed possible that the buck still had a remembrance of the hunter's prior attempted shot. The alarming experience had apparently been imprinted on the buck's brain.

He was more cautious. He seemed to remember. It changed his personality, so to speak.

Whitetails, and most other animals, are often thought to be systematic creatures. Although they don't think and reason like humans, they do react to experiences and change their habits to accommodate various situations on many occasions.

The rut causes unpredictable reactions in most cases. Land changes by farming, timber losses, commercial development of favored habitat affect deer habits. Weather changes alter deer behavior, as well.

Most importantly, hunting pressure can cause deer to avoid habitual travel routes. Interference from human hunters can make a normally patternable buck that would walk right past a hunter, change to a sneaky, unpredictable ghost that plays hide-and-seek with its human pursuer.

Call it what you like: forced reaction to interference, conditioning, coincidence or instinct, but to my mind it makes more sense to label a deer's response as development of a personality. Personality is a trait of mature deer with which researchers and hunters often fail to credit them.

When animal behaviorists try to explain specific types of buck behavior, they revert to the word "instinct." Instinct is a natural attitude; the ability of an animal to perform functions without training. And any experienced deer hunter can tell you that whitetail actions and reactions to different stimuli aren't predictable, as some would lead us to believe. Not everything a buck does is programmed by nature.

The white-tailed buck is an adaptive animal. Still, we can't actually say they are cunning, thinking or creative creatures that plan each day's events, just because they are cautious. Older boss does or mature bucks that have experienced many situations become more sensitive to their environment. They appear to be able to mentally store negative experiences or to "learn" to take advantage of an easier lifestyle. They deal with situations as they arise.

What complicates all of this is that bucks also react to various situations in a manner that is not consistent with past behavior. As human hunters, we think and reason because we are intelligent beings. We can drive a car, read a book or adjust our lives to improve our living standards. We learn from our mistakes as well as our accomplishments.

A human touches a lit match only once and instantly remembers not to do it again because it hurts. Respectively, the buck earlier in this article couldn't have known in reasoning terms that there was a hunter in the tree. He was suspicious, though. And he still shied away from the hunter's stand site even a week later. Maybe not every buck would react this way. This is just one reaction that individualizes this particular white-tailed buck.

It is reasonable to believe that deer don't actually bed down and think about how they will avoid a human hunter the next day. But individual experiences, sensory abilities and stress do control individuality. Each hunter understands that the reactions of each buck will be different from day to day, region to region and animal to animal.

That's why so many successful deer hunters advise tailoring each hunt to conform to terrain, weather conditions, deer mood and the amount of hunting pressure in a given area. Credit for "personality" if not "really thinking" should be given where it's due, and bucks should be hunted accordingly.

There are general hunting methods that will score on many bucks, but we must also be prepared to use unorthodox tactics to bag unorthodox bucks. A specific buck familiarizes itself with its habitat niche, but it's not wired into a sophisticated electronic security system. You can get into his home territory unnoticed if you hunt him as an individual deer.

After that you will need to apply a hunting tactic to accommodate the deer's personality. A buck that is frequently hunted from tree stands gets wise to aerial danger fast. Trip him up by taking to the ground.

Some hunters pick out an ambush spot and are afraid to move, and local bucks walk around and past them daily. Don't be afraid to change locations. Play hop-scotch with a buck to counter his travel moods.

Some bucks walk and sneak while others choose to run for their life. Some bucks stand and stare at you, playing the waiting game. Then you encounter another that has an uncanny ability to sense you, and he tip toes away unnoticed.

There's certainly a difference of opinion between hunters who have first-hand experience with deer in their natural environment and researchers who have dealt with confined deer. Some researchers maintain that deer have set, predictable patterns of behavior. Hunters who have gone one-on-one with experienced bucks maintain that every trophy buck is unique.

Big bucks use "personality" to evade hunters. Personality can be a blend of instinct and response to certain stimuli.

Every experienced deer hunter knows white-tailed bucks don't react on command or in a systematic manner. They do react differently to various situations. Although we can't assume that big bucks can think, they do display a form of personality that makes them individualistic big game animals that can be patterned only with patience and persistence.

2

Let Your Barometer Help You Take More Deer

by Robert L. McKinney

*H*unters have known for centuries that changes in atmospheric pressure make deer alter their patterns of feeding and movement, but it has always been a homespun understanding. We just knew it. Now modern science is beginning to comprehend just exactly how these pressure changes affect deer—and how you can turn this knowledge into trophies.

It's no secret that deer tend to move more right before a storm approaches, sit tight during long periods of rain or snow, and promptly rush out to feed or resume mating activity on the storm's tail end. Just about anyone who has ever spent much time hunting or living in the country knows that.

He or she also has observed that deer (and other animals) seem to have a "sixth sense" about approaching changes in the weather, a sense we now know is really a function of the inner ear's sensitivity to changes in atmospheric (or barometric) pressures. Humans also have this sensitivity, but we've pretty much forgotten it over decades of living in cities, cut off from nature.

We can still take advantage of these changes, however, by learning to use and interpret a barometer and/or barometric weather map. This might sound complicated, but it is not and is a skill that any hunter really needs.

This ability can help us pick the best times to hunt, the best places to hunt, and even allows tailoring our hunting methods to suit the conditions we will be encountering.

But, before we get into all that, let's take a quick look at just what a barometer is and how it works.

How a Barometer Works

First, you must understand that the entire earth is surrounded by an invisible ocean of air. (No, you don't see the air—what you can see is water vapor and pollution!) This layer of air is most dense at the bottom and becomes progressively thinner the higher one gets. It is a fact well understood by every flatlander who has gone out West for his first hunt in the mountains.

The air also gets "thicker" or "thinner" based on a number of other conditions, including temperature and moisture content. For example, cold air is thicker—and thus heavier—than hot air, which is why a balloon filled with heated air rises. (Incidentally, your body heat and odor also rise in higher pressure air, thereby making odor control easier in high pressure conditions than in low pressure conditions, when odor tends to linger on the ground.)

The way we measure "thickness" or "thinness" of air is by actually weighing it with a barometer. Air measured at sea level and at precisely 32 degrees Fahrenheit, will weigh 14.7 pounds per square inch of surface. This is a "standard atmosphere" and is the theoretical norm against which other atmospheric pressures are compared.

Put another way, 14.7 P.S.I. is enough weight of air to lift a column of mercury in a sealed tube 29.92 inches at mean sea level. Since the original barometers (first invented in Italy about 1650) used a sealed tube of mercury, barometric pressure readings are still usually given in "inches of mercury" even though mercury is not used in portable barometers today. Instead of mercury, they use a sealed vacuum chamber.

If you've ever watched a TV weather report, you've heard a lot of talk about areas of high or low pressure, commonly called "highs" or "lows." These areas and their movements are caused by the heating and cooling of our planet by the sun, by prevailing winds, by ocean currents such as the Gulf Stream and by other global factors.

Areas of high pressure generally include clear skies with no precipitation. "Lows," on the other hand, often feature precipitation. This is basically because the "thick," cooler air of a high pressure area can hold more moisture in suspension without becoming saturated than can the thinner air in a low pressure area.

Breeding activity can stop as whitetails pause for foul weather.

As long as you're in a "high," skies will stay clear and precipitation-free (except for late-afternoon thunderstorms). Conversely, when a low-pressure system is overhead, things will remain cloudy and it will continue to stay gloomy or rain or snow.

The real action begins when these pressure systems, either high or low, pack up and begin moving—because that's when game activity also increases.

Game Moves When The Barometer Does

As long as atmospheric pressure holds steady or is changing very slowly—whether it be high, normal or low—game activity remains relatively stable as well. For example, as long as the barometric pressure stays the same, the big "unkillable" bucks seldom venture into the open until all the shooting light is gone, and they disappear well before the morning hunter can see to shoot. If your hunting area is in a stalled pressure system, especially if there is relatively constant rain or snow, you can expect little movement.

In times like these, you will be forced to either go to the game—

it won't be coming to you—or use some other method of forcing it to move. This might be a good time to do a little still hunting, try glassing and stalking or organize a drive.

When the barometer starts to move rapidly up or down, however, everything changes! Suddenly the woods and fields become alive with animals as they scurry about looking for food to break their fast or to stock up for the bad weather their instincts tell them is coming. There's no need for the hunter to move now—just sit tight and let the animals come to you!

Sexual activity such as rubbing, scraping, sparring and actual mating also increases when the barometer begins to change, especially if the barometric change is upward. Clearing weather prior to or during the rut will have bucks fanning out from their safe areas to make up for lost time as they feverishly freshen scrapes and look for receptive does. This means that if the hunter has located an active scrape, the time to get on stand is the second that barometer begins to head upward—or before!

A rapidly falling barometer, on the other hand, usually indicates there will be a storm in less than 24 hours, and has the greatest effect of all on game movement. This is true not only for deer, but for elk, bear, small game, and even upland birds and waterfowl as well. Their natural barometers tell them they'd better take care of any pending business, find a safe haven in which to wait out the storm and fill their stomachs with food to get them through whatever nasty weather is approaching.

One special note: look for animals out feeding where they usually do. Don't get the idea that just because they are feeding at an "odd" time, they will also feed at a new or unusual place. With a storm coming, they want to stock their stomachs as quickly as possible, so they will go to where they already know there's food. If bucks have been frequenting a particular alfalfa field, that's where to look for them.

Whitetails Are Extra-Sensitive To Barometric Pressures

The effects of a falling barometer on white-tailed deer has been especially well documented. According to *White-tailed Deer: Ecology and Management* from the Wildlife Management Institute, a number of researchers in widely separated states have all reported evidence of maximum deer movement when atmospheric pressure was falling rapidly.

F.B. Barick, a North Carolina researcher, for example, reported that he "was able to increase trapping success greatly by setting deer traps when the barometer was falling, with a forecast of rain or snow within 24 hours." Barick reported that "…in one area I was able to catch 68 deer in four nights by trapping ahead of storm fronts, compared with only 65 deer captured in (the same area during a 10-week period the previous year.)"

A rapidly moving barometer also has a significant effect on mules and elk. Both vary their ranges in response to weather, especially if temperatures and other meteorological conditions are also rapidly changing. A falling barometer coupled with increasing winds and decreasing temperatures at high elevations often starts mules, elk, and even whitetails working down the mountains as they look for warmer air and shelter from the wind. A rising barometer frequently has the opposite effect. A good rule of thumb is to hunt lower if that's the way the barometer is heading and higher if the opposite is true.

Although the Weather Channel on cable TV provides good information, hunters who rely on the local TV station to report the weather or who wait until they actually see the weather changing or the game beginning to move have already missed the boat. In the field, of course, you won't have access to all the equipment available to professional meteorologists, but with a little bit of experience you can use your barometer to pick the best hunting times. Just remember, game moves when the barometer does. The faster the barometer needle is swinging, the more active the game. Especially if the barometer has held steady for several days, the second it does begin moving, grab your gear and head for the woods!

An even better way of predicting barometric changes is to study what are known as barometric weather maps. These are weather maps that show barometric pressures in lines that look very similar to the contour lines on a topographic map. Such maps are sometimes available in better daily newspapers, but the best sources include the flight service center at your local airport or offices of the U.S. Weather Service (usually located at the nearest airport big enough to have regular airline service).

To accurately predict how the barometric pressures are changing, you'll need to study the map, keeping in mind that high and low pressure systems tend to surge in pretty much the same way as do waves on a beach. By comparing barometric pressure maps from the past two or three days, you will be able to pick up the pattern. Barometric pressure maps are usually issued every 12 hours.

Barometric Pressures Affect Wind

High and low pressure systems are much like giant cyclones, usually covering several states at once, but they can be anywhere from small local cells the size of a county to giant systems that can cover most of the United States and part of Canada and Mexico.

In the Northern Hemisphere, the air of a low-pressure system rotates counterclockwise, while a high-pressure system spins clockwise. This means that if you face into the prevailing wind, the low pressure system will be on your right. As either type of system passes over you, the winds will decrease the closer you get to the "eye" of the system, then change direction 180 degrees and begin to increase as the system moves on. As the center of the system passes over you, your barometer will also reverse direction.

How fast the winds change direction and speed and how fast the barometer changes direction will all depend upon the speed of the system across the ground. Also, by observing which way your barometer's needle is moving, you can tell if you are heading into higher or lower pressure.

How to Choose a Barometer for Hunting

Decent barometers are available from several sources. Prices range from about $10 to hundreds. There's no need to spend the family fortune; just be sure you buy one that's easy to read, rugged, and if it's portable, so much the better.

3

How Deer See Hunters

by Larry Weishuhn

What do white-tailed deer see when they encounter a hunter in the woods? Do they see merely a shape which blends in with the surroundings? Or, do they see a bright form like a beacon in the night?

These questions have long been on deer hunters' minds, really, since the original research on hunter blaze orange was conducted.

Previously the initials UV were primarily the concern of sun worshippers. UV is the harmful band of light that does the most damage to human skin.

Then, suddenly, UV became the key letters in almost every deer hunter's vocabulary. Other new words included "ultraviolet," "wavelength," "UV Killer" and "Sports Wash."

Could deer see colors the same as we do, or only colors in the ultraviolet spectrum? Some experts agreed with all the new information; others did not. Some hunters swore by the new products; others swore at them. The questions continued.

Many wildlife biologists who have worked with whitetails questioned some of the research—especially when we learned the original "what deer see" work was done on hogs rather than white-tailed deer. It was assumed hogs and deer had similar eye structure and vision capabilities. Some of us also thought there was far too much emphasis being placed on new products and theories rather than good woodsmanship and basic hunting skills.

Be that as it may, there is some new research which will be of interest to those who are concerned with what deer are reputed to see. In a technical paper given at the 16th Annual Southeast Deer Study Group meeting, a team of researchers from the University of Georgia presented their results.

The paper, "Photopigments of White-Tailed Deer," was co-authored by Brian P. Murphy, Karl Miller and R. Larry Machinton with the University of Georgia; Jess Deegan II with the University of California; Jay Neitz, Medical College of Wisconsin; and Gerald H. Jacobs of the University of California.

Quoting from the paper's abstract, "All aspects of vision depend ultimately on the absorption of light by photopigments. The retinas of white-tailed deer, like those of other ungulates, contain a mixture of rod and cone photoreceptors."

To paraphrase their research procedure, they used a noninvasive electrophysiological technique to measure the spectral absorption properties of the photopigments contained within the deer's eye. In other words, it was an attempt to determine what deer see by using sophisticated equipment and techniques.

Light-evoked potentials were sensed by a contact lens electrode positioned on the eye of anesthetized deer. Again to quote, "The eye was stimulated with a rapidly-pulsed, monochromatic light: variations in pulse rate, stimulus wavelength and adaptation state of the eye allowed preferential access to signals from different classes of photoreceptors. Recordings were obtained from nine white-tailed deer. Three classes of photopigment were detected. One of these is the photopigment contained in rods; it has peak sensitivity of about 496 nm, a value greatly similar to that found for rod photopigments in other mammals. These measurements also reveal the presence of two classes of cone. One contains a photopigment maximally sensitive in the middle wavelengths; the other cone class has a sensitivity peak in the short wavelengths. In light of what is known about the relationship between photopigments and vision in other species, these results suggest two likely characteristics of cone-based (i.e., daylight) vision in deer: (1) deer should be relatively less sensitive to long wavelength lights than other mammals, (i.e., humans) and (2) white-tailed deer would be expected to have dichromatic color vision."

So what does all that scientific jargon mean to us deer hunters? First of all, it means the most recent research was performed on

Scientific studies leave questions about white-tailed clear vision and color recognition capabilities unanswered.

white-tailed deer. That, at least, is refreshing.

Some of the latest research questions how "real" deer perceive UV brighteners in camouflage, blaze orange and other garments. According to a research report from Atsko, Inc., a manufacturer of garment cleaning products, to apply what has been learned about visual systems of deer, one must determine under what ambient light the garment is viewed.

In direct sunlight at high noon, there are longer wavelengths and we humans see no effect from U-V brighteners. As the Earth rotates and light conditions change toward dusk or dawn, or on days of heavy overcast skies or dark shade, the amount of UV and short blue light decreases; meanwhile "the fraction of total light contributed by UV increases greatly," according to a report by Atsko's Dan Gutting. "These periods coincide with peak whitetail activity."

According to Gutting's report, humans would see such effects only on white or light-colored garments. Deer, however, should be able to see these same effects on almost any color. But even with deer, the surroundings of what they are looking at is important. Gutting's report says natural foliage is deficient in blue and UV wavelengths. It says other variations such as motion, pattern size, specular reflectance, and brightness in long wavelengths are also important, but in the report these factors were neglected because humans are capable of observing and correcting them.

That's an interesting way of discussing hunting basics.

According to Atsko, if you wash your hunting clothes in a "brighter-brights washing detergent" it may contain fluorescent whitening agents. These whitening agents release energy they gathered through the UV spectrum in small bands of short blue wavelengths.

According to the Atsko report, "Deer are much more sensitive than humans to the shorter wavelengths of light. Deer have a blue cone which picks up light most humans cannot see. This light is perceived as bright blue in the dichromatic (two color) eye of the deer. This light occurs on garments of any color, from camouflage to blaze orange if brighteners are present."

In a paper presented by Dr. Jay Neitz to the International Hunter Education Association, he said deer have two cones that allow them to see blue and yellow. But then he continued by saying deer lack photoreceptors for seeing the differences in the colors of objects that reflect yellow-greens, green, yellow, orange and red. He then said deer should be relatively less sensitive to long-wavelengths light (orange and red especially) than humans.

Reportedly, under low light conditions deer switch to using rods (used to see black, white and shades of gray). At that point the light mentioned above is supposedly perceived by deer as a bright gray. We humans see color better than deer in poor light conditions.

Deer lack the red cones we have. This suggests they do not see reds. Therefore, if blaze orange has not had any brighteners applied, deer should not see the brightness of the orange as well as humans see it.

White-tailed deer, according to the University of Georgia research, are expected to have dichromatic color vision, not unlike some humans who are color blind and lack the red cones. Humans with that form of color blindness see blues as blues and the rest of the color spectrum from green to red as the color yellow. Thus—and here is where it gets interesting—deer should perceive blaze orange and most of the green/brown camouflage without brighteners as the color yellow.

Why is that important and doubly interesting? Again, if the research is correct then blaze orange and green/brown camouflage patterns without brighteners would blend in with the world of green and yellow leaves, green and yellowish-brown grass, green trees and brown tree trunks, because all these would be seen as yellows by deer. In the case of blaze orange, fellow hunters can readily see it, but the hunter wearing it would not be seen in the same way by deer.

While this research seems to confirm what the folks at Atsko, Inc. have been saying all along, it also points out the importance of good woodsmanship, slow movement and attempts by hunters to try to blend in with their background and surroundings. A lack of brighteners in or on our hunting clothes or the blaze orange that we wear while afield might prevent us from being quite as visible to deer. But it is not an excuse for sloppy hunting techniques.

Am I fully convinced by the research? Three years ago I was quoted in one of the *NAH* articles as saying, "The jury is still out." The latest research is an excellent bit of evidence in favor of using UV control solutions. Chances are excellent I'll start paying a little more attention to the hunting clothes I wear and how deer perceive the colors and brighteners used to manufacture the clothes.

But, I'll also strive to wear soft clothing that blends in with my surroundings, move slowly, keep the breeze in my face and the sun at my back.

4

Deer On The Moon

by Jeff Murray

*T*oo cold. Too hot. Not enough rain. Too wet. Not enough bucks. Too many antlerless permits. Must have happened last week. Too bad I have to work next week.

Why all the excuses for not scoring during the whitetail rut? This is supposed to be a can't-miss period in the fall. After all, it's been discussed, dissected and diagnosed more than any other subject in the whitetail world—even novice hunters know that just prior to breeding is when bucks are most vulnerable.

The main problem here lies with the fickle nature of the rut. One year it seems to peak early, the next year it hits two weeks late. Sometimes it hits like lightning for a couple of days—when you couldn't get out, of course—and other times it trickles along largely unnoticed. Then, just when you conclude the rut is a memory, a buddy exclaims, "You shoulda seen all the bucks on the move the other day!"

Needless to say, the ability to accurately predict peak rutting activity would be a tremendous breakthrough for hunters. Knowing exactly when bucks are most likely to throw caution to the wind, as they run on testosterone overdrive, focusing on receptive females, should bump the odds up considerably.

It might sound too good to be true, but I believe this goal is easily attainable. You won't need a crystal ball, and you don't have to give in to the power of the Dark Side. The secret belongs to the moon.

How credible is this new revelation? Frankly, I've found it to be dead-on in my experiments, and one Michigan bowhunter I know has predicted the rut accurately for nearly a decade. The good news is that anyone can do the same with a relatively simple formula that not only measures the timing of the rut, but also its intensity and duration.

"I've been bowhunting for more than 20 years, and ever since I can remember I've kept a log on the moon and related rutting activity," Michigan bowhunter Bob Scriver told me. "I'm absolutely convinced that the new moon is the key [for setting] the rut."

Rut Science 101

Before we get into the details, let's review a few basic facts about the whitetail's reproductive cycle. First, does entering estrus actually determine peak breeding activity? Bucks are ready to breed long before traditional rutting dates, but dominant breeding bucks that have been around the block don't get very antsy until they get a whiff of the first does entering estrus.

Second, photoperiodism—the diminishing ratio of daylight to darkness—triggers the onset of the reproductive cycle. Just as a buck's antlers begin to form when longer days signal its pituitary gland to release testosterone, a doe undergoes a similar transformation in the fall. As the days become shorter, her pineal gland releases melatonin, a substance influencing the release of sex hormones from the pituitary. The pineal gland acts as a translator of photoperiod clues, and this is where the new moon—the phase when the moon cannot be seen and the night sky is as dark as it gets—comes in.

Third, we need to differentiate "peak of the rut" from "peak breeding."

"The first is when the average hunter thinks deer are hyperactive," says Texas wildlife biologist Bob Zaiglin. "The second is when the majority of does are actually being bred. The peak of the rut occurs when bucks aggressively search for does, typically just before most of them come into estrus, or just after estrus has been terminated. 'Peak breeding,' on the other hand, might actually be a relatively benign period, as far as hunting excitement goes. We've examined embryos in the spring down in South Texas to back-date conception periods, and they don't always jibe with when we've seen the most bucks the previous fall."

In other words, from a hunting perspective, we're most interested in the very beginning of the estrus cycle.

Lunar Effects On Does

Is it coincidence that the doe's heat cycle and the lunar cycle are both 28 days? Indeed, the moon's face-to-face cycle, or lunation, is 29.5 days. Its sidereal cycle (completion of rotation around the Earth) is 27.3 days, thus, the average is 28.4 days. Moreover, studies on the heat cycle of does revealed spans of 28 and 29 days between successive cycles in New York; 21 to 27 days in Upper Michigan; and 25 to 30 days in Minnesota.

Inconsistent "rut dates" from fall to fall are caused by the new moon landing on different days during rutting months, Scriver maintains.

"A doe's pineal gland doesn't just measure waning sunlight, but it responds to all light, including that of the moon," he says. "Suppose a new moon arrives earlier than a traditional rutting date for a given

New Moon Dates

Year	October	November	December
1993	10-15	11-13	12-13
1994	10-5	11-3	12-2
1995	10-24	11-22	12-22
1996	10-12	11-11	12-10
1997	10-31	11-30	12-29
1998	10-20	11-19	12-18
1999	10-9	11-8	12-7

deer population. The peak rut will be skewed ahead of schedule.

"The doe's pineal gland tells [its pituitary gland] that the light is less, so the day must be shorter. Estrogen levels then increase, and she cycles. Poultry farmers have artificially manipulated light levels to enhance egg production for years. So has the Michigan DNR when attempting to boost pheasant production. It's no big deal."

A case in point was 1994's new moon date of November 3. I remember that date well, because I was fortunate to draw a non-resident bow tag for Kansas whitetails. I had been scout-hunting for several days with very few deer sightings under my belt.

The main reason for the suppressed activity was a combination of unusually hot weather and 35 mph southeast winds. Then bingo! As soon as the new moon hit, my hunting partner and I witnessed a sudden frenzy of bucks chasing does. In fact, we got a good look at the Pope and Young buck I was after as he skirted a patch of brush right during the middle of the day. The 75-degree heat didn't seem to bother him one bit as he panted after a flirting doe.

New Moon Formula

The "optimum length of day" is the starting point for determining traditional rutting dates. Once a doe's pineal gland determines daylight and darkness are in agreement, she cycles. This general period varies from region to region. For example, in higher latitudes the rut typically peaks earlier because daylight is shorter. Areas with heavy snowfall are an exception to the rule as fawns must be born during favorable spring conditions. Another example includes flood plains—the rutting season is delayed to allow does to drop fawns after swelling water levels subside in the spring.

Genetic differences in some states—Texas has three distinct rut dates, Alabama four or more—force hunters to stay on their toes. Naturally, state and provincial biologists keep track of these variations and maintain records on traditional rutting dates for their jurisdiction. But without the moonlight factor, which can make the day seem longer or shorter to a doe, no biologist can tell you when's the best time to go hunting.

The Formula

You can compute this on your own by first comparing how a particular lunation overlaps a traditional peak rut date. To predict future rut hunts, here's the formula. If a new moon:

* Is "on time," thus coinciding with optimum daylight for estrus release: The rut will be electrifying for a rather short spell. The length of day is ideal for peak rutting, and so is the darkness of the moon. The frenzy will quickly subside, however, as the majority of does are bred and go out of estrus.

* Hits late: Most hunters will complain of a sub-par rut, but chase activity will occur a week later, after a lot of hunters have given up prematurely. In states with firearms seasons overlapping the peak breeding season—Michigan, Minnesota, Wisconsin—many bucks

will be harvested with few remaining to service late-estrus does. Fewer does bred in November, therefore, can lead to an accelerated second rut in December.

* Arrives a week early: The rut should be "decent," according to Scriver, arriving earlier and maintaining a fairly even keel. But if the rut's two weeks early, like it was in 1994 (November 3), rutting activity hits a moderate level but lacks intensity. "Naturally, the nights are darker, but the days aren't yet short enough to result in peak activity," Scriver says. "The net effect is no change translated through the pineal gland. By the traditional rut date of, say, November 15, daylight will be short enough to trigger a trickling rut that will be diluted."

Don't forget the weather, either. A prolonged spell of thunderstorms and dark, overcast skies during the fall suppresses general deer activity. "I believe weather depresses deer much as it does humans," Scriver says. "So a day or two after the clouds lift, bucks often go bonkers; they've been cooped up at a time when they're used to being free spirits, and a few does coming into a short period of heat will trigger a brief whirlwind of breeding. This false heat will quickly reverse itself, however, so you really have to stay on top of it."

See the chart on page 27 for a few new moons to back-date and some to think about for future rut-oriented hunts:

Full Moon's Midday Frenzy

There are two kinds of rattlers in Texas—snakes and antler-bangers. If you don't want to be lumped into the former camp, you better learn the real secret to rattling the most dominant breeding bucks in your area. It boils down to waiting for a full moon to overlap the main rut.

"During the rut, bucks push does out in [cactus] flats, running them ragged," Zaiglin says. "By sunrise, the does will be holed up, and around midday they need to get up, stretch and go to feed. Meanwhile, bucks continue pestering them. The typical three-day period of an estrus doe is no time to slack off at midday. Over the years, I and many of my clients have taken some impressive trophies at this time."

Which leads to the most important reason why trophy hunters like Dick Idol, David Morris and Charlie Alsheimer concentrate on this lunar period: The demand for does exceeds the supply. Since most of the does will have been triggered earlier, during the new moon, now, two weeks later, very few of them will be in heat.

Competition is keen.

No wonder rattling is a bust during the peak breeding season—when the supply of hot does is at its peak—but a week or two later hunters are often able to raise the hackles of a buck.

"The buck's ornery because it's been a while since he's had any action," Scriver says. "He's been running for nights, and no doe will stand for him. He's on edge. Rattling when a full moon overlaps the rut can be deadly, if you hit it just right."

Which, thanks to the Man in the Moon, isn't as elusive as it used to be. Remember the new moon formula, and you could plan the best deer hunt of your life.

Earthly Factors

The new moon isn't the only factor determining the specific days of the breeding season. A few other keys unlock the rut mystery. One is the weather.

Contrary to popular belief, a sudden cold snap isn't what coaxes neutral bucks into first (or second) gear. Periods of dark, overcast weather followed by a bright sky is. Watch weather trends and especially note cloud conditions. You could time a hunt to coincide with a short flurry of activity by hunting immediately following a cold front; the first day or two of sunshine could be dynamite.

Research at the University of Georgia reveals that the quality of the mast crop during a particular year substantially impacts antler development. This, in turn, affects rubbing activity—poor mast crop, few rubs. And fewer rubs in a particular habitat mean less "priming pheromones" available to condition does to cycle. (Experiments have shown that the presence—or absence—of males can affect the timing of female estrus cycles.)

Additionally, deer populations with young bucks doing most of the breeding (where hunting pressure is intense or quality deer management is lacking) lead to less rubbing activity, and this also means fewer priming pheromones to trigger does to cycle early. Translation: All other factors remaining equal, if the number of buck rubs in your hunting area seems to be down, the rut could be delayed slightly.

Finally, droughts severely curtail general buck activity, mainly because antler development is hampered. Again, fewer rubs will appear in the deer woods, and this means fewer does will be "primed" for an early estrus.

5

Daytime Deer From Moon Shadows

by Dr. Grant Woods

*U*nless you are among the lucky few who can hunt whenever the urge strikes, planning when to hunt is as important as where to hunt. Most hunters must schedule their hunts weeks or even months in advance. They usually plan to hunt during the rut or when preferred deer food sources will be available. Although breeding dates and food source timing are important considerations, they may not be the best criteria for scheduling a hunt.

Because deer might breed and feed at night, the key is knowing when deer will be most active during daylight hours. Hunting in the vicinity of great sign will not compensate for nocturnal deer activity.

One of my long-term research projects involved studying deer behavior associated with large rubs. To ensure "real world" results, the study was conducted in an area that received heavy hunting pressure. Activity-triggered cameras were used to photograph deer near rubs.

The photographs revealed that only a small percentage of the rub activity occurred during daylight hours. Nothing is more frustrating than hunting over great sign and failing to see deer.

Many hunters know there will be a surge of deer activity just before the first strong cold front of the season. I always try to pick a stand near a preferred food source and hunt just before that initial cold front passes. However, the weather is not reliably predictable weeks, or even days, in advance; and therefore, can seldom can be used to plan a hunt.

As a result, I began trying to identify predictable factors that influence daytime deer activity. Like many researchers and writers, I initially studied the effectiveness of two moon orbit characteristics that are frequently used to predict daylight deer activity—moon phase (new, waxing, full and waning) and moon position (overhead or underfoot). These two characteristics have probably been used so often for prediction because they are easily observed by the naked eye.

Many outdoors people are aware of these through the "lunar tables" published to predict fish and game feeding times. The moon's gravity pulls on large bodies of water and causes two high tides each day—one when the moon is directly overhead and the other when the moon is underfoot (on the far side of the earth). This gravitational pull on water is thought to influence feeding behavior.

However, this theory neglects to consider how deer differ from fish. A deer's diet is composed of plants, while most game fish are predators. Although the moon's gravitational effect on water might increase bait fish activity and trigger feeding behavior in predator fish, it does not affect when a deer's food source will be available.

A few previous scientific research results have shown there is no relationship between daylight deer activity and moon phases. Hunters everywhere now realize deer are influenced by the moon's position.

The Next Level Of Lunar Pull

To learn more about the moon, I began working with a national astronomical observatory, obtaining data on several additional characteristics of the moon's orbit. To my knowledge, these characteristics had not previously been compared to daytime deer activity. Two of these characteristics are the moon's declination (angle north or south of the Earth's equator) and its distance from the Earth's surface. These orbit patterns change daily, but the variations cannot be seen by the naked eye.

During 1991, I started a research project on a 6,000-acre property in South Carolina that required the observation and harvest of wild, free-ranging deer. The Mount Holly project was designed to demon-strate sound deer management strategies by balancing the adult sex ratio and allowing bucks to survive to mature age classes. Hence the goal was to harvest several does and a limited quota of mature bucks; immature bucks were passed.

Observation and harvest data were collected predominantly by wildlife biologists with a doctorate or master's degree to ensure all necessary biological and observation data were recorded. These biologists harvested deer by using standard hunting techniques, primarily hunting from tree stands, and followed all state regulations and fair chase guidelines. Stand sites were usually near seasonal food sources (primarily acorns) and travel corridors. Rattling, grunt calls, decoys and various other techniques were used.

During four hunting seasons at Mount Holly these researchers observed 2,900 wild, free-ranging deer and harvested 435.

This provided an unparalleled set of observation data to compare with moon orbit characteristics for predicting daytime deer activity. I used statistical tests to determine if the astronomical data could be used to accurately predict days with the greatest daytime deer activity. The results showed that certain moon orbit characteristics, including declination and distance between the moon and earth, accurately predicted days when daytime deer activity was greatest.

The Formula Develops

Based on the statistical analysis, I divided the moon data into seven classes. Each class represents a predicted level of daytime deer activity. A "10" indicates the highest level of activity and a "4" the lowest (even on low activity days, there will be some movement). Because these research results provided an accurate index for predicting deer activity, the project has been named the Deer Activity Index or DAI.

Once I understood the moon's effect on daytime deer activity, I used the DAI to schedule hunts at the Mount Holly project for 1995. South Carolina's deer season is long and bag limits are liberal, but the researchers had to travel 200 miles to the project site. Since most of the biologists have "real" jobs with agencies or universities, some hunts were scheduled during holidays. During 1995, many of the holiday hunts occurred on days with low DAI numbers of 4 or 5. Other hunts were purposely scheduled for days with a DAI class of 8 or higher.

For the 1995 season, 422 hunts were required to harvest the number of deer mandated by the project's parameters. A hunt was considered a full morning or afternoon; a full day of hunting equaled two hunts. During the hunts, each researcher recorded the amount of time spent hunting and the number of bucks, does, fawns and unidentified deer observed.

To ensure the data accurately reflected deer activity, it was required that a minimum of four researchers hunt at the same time from different stand locations. To determine the level of deer activity for each hunt, the total number of deer observed by the researchers was divided by the total number of minutes spent in the stand. Using an average of several hunters' observations provided a more accurate measure of deer activity than the observations of a single hunter. This reduced the effects of an individual hunter not seeing any deer because of poor stand location, poachers, predators or other uncontrollable events in the area.

Before the 1995 season, I published my predictions of daytime deer activity for each DAI class based on the volume of earlier data and strength of the statistics. These are shown in the chart below.

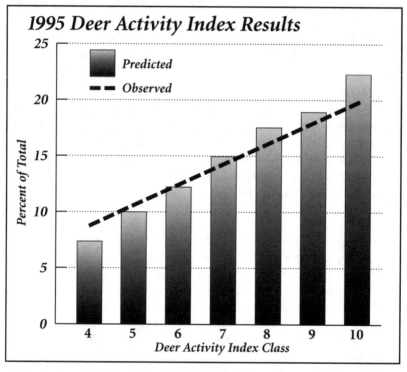

For example, I predicted deer would be almost twice as active during daylight on "9" days than on "5" days. For hunting purposes, this would mean a hunter would have to hunt two days with a DAI class of "5" to see as many deer as on a one-day hunt with a DAI class of "9."

Also shown in the graph are the results of a statistical analysis of the actual 1995 observation data from the Mount Holly project (a linear regression with an R2 of 0.43 for you statistically oriented hunters). During 1995, the researchers at the Mount Holly project observed 640 deer during 1,134 hours of stand time. The researchers averaged observing 76 percent more deer on "8," "9," and "10" (high DAI) days than on "4," "5," and "6" (low DAI) days.

To ensure these results were not limited to South Carolina, several wildlife biologists and large hunting clubs throughout the whitetail's range also monitored the number of deer they observed. Data from these sources reflected the same trends. One example was the Weller Mountain Hunt Club located in the Adirondack Mountains of New York. Weller Mountain has 130 members and several guests each year. The deer season in the Adirondacks runs from late September through early December with the bulk being a firearms season. The two common hunting techniques at Weller Mountain are stand hunting and drives.

Based on the observation data collected by stand hunters at Weller Mountain, 54 percent more deer were observed on "8," "9," and "10" days compared to "4," "5," and "6" days. Although these results were impressive, the drive hunting results were also interesting.

Hunters that participated in drive hunts observed 26 percent more deer on high DAI days compared to low DAI days. Because drive hunts are designed to "push" deer and do not rely on natural deer activity, I did not anticipate the data to show such a significant difference between high and low DAI days for the drive hunts.

The data collected during the 1995 season confirmed the DAI's accuracy. As a scientist, and as a deer hunter, it was rewarding to receive positive feedback from fellow hunters and other researchers throughout the whitetail's range.

Combine With Good Hunting Basics

The DAI does not indicate where to hunt, but rather when to hunt to maximize deer observations. Hunters should use their knowledge of food availability, hunting pressure and habitat type to determine where to hunt. These factors vary greatly, depending on location and season.

A stand in an oak flat that was productive during October, 1993, when the stomach content averaged 43 percent acorns, was probably not productive during October, 1995, when the average stomach content was only 3.2 percent acorns.

The weather is even less predictable than the availability of preferred food sources. During one Mount Holly hunting trip, the DAI numbers were high ("8" or above) and so was the deer activity. The researchers were observing almost twice as many deer per hour compared to a hunt two weeks before that was scheduled on days with DAI numbers of "4" and "5."

On the third day of the hunt, a weather front passed causing very strong winds during the afternoon. Although it was a "9" day and several deer had been harvested that morning, very few deer were observed during the afternoon hunt. Abnormal climatic conditions might occasionally outweigh the DAI.

DAI Doesn't Determine Rut

The DAI does not determine when the rut will occur. However, when the peak of the rut occurs during a low DAI period, most of the rub and scrape behavior will be nocturnal. This might explain why hunters frequently comment, "There was not much of a rut this year," or "I hunted near several fresh rubs and scrapes, but did not see many deer."

The DAI also does not replace sound hunting techniques. However, it does allow hunters and researchers to plan their field time on days that are prone to have high levels of daytime deer activity. This is especially important for those who have limited opportunities to be in the woods. Food availability and weather conditions cannot be predicted. However, the DAI can be used to predict the best days to schedule time afield.

References

Harlow, R. F., and W. F. Oliver, Jr. 1967. Natural factors affecting deer movement. Q. J. Fla. Acad. Sci. 30(3):221-226.

Michael, E. D. 1970. Activity patterns of white-tailed deer in south Texas. Tex. J. Sci. XXI(4):417-428.

Woods, G. R. 1994. Studies on traditional rubs and the human dimensions associated with quality deer management. Ph.D. dissertation., Clemson University. 72 pp.

Woods, G. R. 1995. Beyond moon phases: Deer and Deer Hunting. (two part series) 18(8):19-26, 19(1):16-24.

6

Can The Experts Count On Infrared?

by Charles Bridwell

Wildlife management has not always been in sync with the times, but some states are now using Space Age technology to count deer and other game animals from the air.

One of the greatest challenges vexing wildlife managers has always been getting accurate census data on individual species, especially those that are prone to overpopulation. Deer biologists have for years relied on counting tracks along roadways, pellet counts, using spotlights at night to count animals in forest and field, and even aerial flights during periods of snow cover.

Today there's a new method being tested that could provide a clearer vision of deer population estimating, at least in some parts of the country.

Infrared technology is not new. It's been used by the military for years and was originally used to detect troops at night. Infrared locates the subtle radiation of body heat in animals and projects an outline or ghost image onto a monitor screen.

The first attempts to use infrared for counting wildlife came in the early 1960s. Studies were done in 1968 and 1972 to determine the accuracy of infrared, but the technology was still shrouded by military secrecy, and much of the best equipment was considered top secret. Only recently did the government release enough technology to make infrared a viable tool for wildlife managers.

Tests in Missouri seek to determine the real accuracy of infrared as a deer population estimating tool. The studies also look for ways to enhance accuracy. Lonnie Hansen, wildlife research biologist and deer program leader for Missouri's Department of Wildlife, began the study in 1993. It is a cooperative project between the Missouri Department of Conservation and the University of Missouri.

Deer were trapped and collared with metallic collars that could be detected with infrared from an airplane or helicopter. The collars also had radio transmitters. The plan was to locate deer by the radio signal, then test the infrared's ability to detect the deer using varying altitudes, speeds, types of aircraft, and varying flight patterns, called transects. "Our goal was to establish parameters that would result in the greatest accuracy with infrared," Hansen said.

"The problem we're running into," he continued, "is that many states are using the method with varying rates of success. They're missing many of the deer. In some of our tests, spotlight counts revealed there were many more deer in the test are than indicated by infrared. We even tried a computer program that read a videotape of the monitor during the flight. It was supposed to remove human bias, since there's a lot of interpretation possible in reading an infrared screen. But we found the computer program also removed human judgment and was not very accurate. It vastly under-counted the deer."

Traditional Census Methods

In theory, infrared first appears to be a panacea for wildlife biologists. To get an accurate count of deer in a specific area by flying overhead and viewing a monitor would greatly reduce the man-hours spent using pellet counts or searching for deer with spotlights along roadways. Other methods that estimate deer numbers based on population dynamics and data fed into the program, such as harvest statistics and age, weight and sex ratios, have their proponents, but are often doubted by hunters and the general public. Seeing is believing.

"One of our principle methods of counting deer in the past was by counting them from a helicopter after a snowfall," Hansen said. "They're very easy to spot against the white background when the leaves are off the trees. The problem is, we don't get snow in all areas every year, and many states don't get snow at all."

Why Count Deer Anyway?

Why is counting deer so important?

"The count helps us substantiate our hunting and management decisions statewide," Hansen said. "Missouri is a pretty rural state, and we're not under as much pressure as some eastern states to justify management, but more and more, wildlife agencies are facing pressures from animal-rights and anti-hunting groups to justify their management decisions and hunting seasons. We want to provide test data that will eliminate as much error as possible."

Hansen said researchers might also attempt to use infrared in summer to fly over fields and attempt to establish doe/fawn or buck/doe relationships. He says that under some conditions infrared can give researchers an idea of deer body size and even show antlers on bucks.

Infrared was also being tested in Arkansas to verify elk numbers on the state's small herd along the Buffalo National River. "We did some infrared last year on our elk herd and counted 312 animals in February and early March," said Mike Cartwright, deer and elk program coordinator for the Arkansas Game and Fish Commission. Cartwright said Arkansas uses harvest data and computer modeling to estimate deer numbers.

Kentucky and Georgia essentially use these same techniques, while other states like South Carolina and Virginia rely more on the physical condition of the deer to provide insight into the balance between deer numbers and available habitat.

"I maintain that knowing deer numbers is not essential to managing them," says Darrell Shipes, assistant chief of wildlife for the South Carolina Department of Natural Resources.

However, there are societal factors like property damage and car-deer collisions that deer managers also must balance. "We have areas where we could carry more deer and maintain them in good health, but culturally speaking, I don't think the public would put up with that many deer in those areas," said Jim Bowman, wildlife biologist for the Virginia Department of Game and Inland Fisheries.

With white-tailed deer populations expanding across much of the animal's range, the matter of cultural carrying capacity is becoming almost equally important as ecological carrying capacity. And so, deer managers will continue to search for new ways to determine how many deer are "out there."

7

Should We Shoot Spikes?

by Larry L. Weishuhn

Despite years of debate, a burning questions persists among white-tailed deer hunters. Should we shoot the spikes to remove them from the gene pool, or should we let 'em walk and let 'em grow?

This question is one of the most frequently asked at the deer management and hunting seminars I present around the country. The answers I give vary, because it really depends on what the hunter or landowner hopes to achieve.

For this discussion, we'll consider spikes deer to be at least 1½ years old with one point or main beam on each side. Before deciding whether or not to shoot spikes, there are some questions you should ask yourself and those folks who hunt with you. What are your long-term goals in terms of deer numbers and the quality of the antlers you'd like the bucks in the herd to produce? Do you want a lot of bucks with average antlers, or would you settle for fewer deer, larger-antlered bucks and an overall healthier deer herd?

If the consensus is that you want higher populations of deer and are not really concerned about antler size, you should probably be passing up spike bucks and allowing them to grow for another year or two. However, if you are interested in improving the quality of the bucks and the deer herd in your area, shoot the spikes. Another, ongoing study backs this up.

Wildlife biologists Donnie Harmel, Bill Armstrong and numerous others working at the Kerr Wildlife Management Area in Texas have been continuously researching the effects of nutrition and genetics on antler development in white-tailed deer. The study began in 1973. Over all these years the researchers have developed a pedigreed, quality-tested deer herd.

Since the inception of the program, each fawn has been tagged and identified relative to sire and dam. The research has taken numerous avenues based on a lot of questions dealing with the effects of nutrition and genetics on antler development.

The initial research demonstrated young bucks frequently develop spike antlers if they are nutritionally deprived during the early stages of life. "Nutritionally deprived" for the purposes of the study was defined as deer sustained with 8 percent or less protein in their diets. In subsequent research, the biologists learned that bucks that started out as spikes seldom caught up in antler development to those bucks that produced forked antlers as yearlings (1½ years of age). Principles of nutrition, genetics and age and their effects on antler growth are the same throughout the whitetail's range.

A primary reason northern white-tailed yearling bucks develop only spikes is a lack of proper nutrition during the all-important first year of their lives. Often this is caused by winter severity. These northern yearling spikes, like their southern counterparts, will eventually develop larger antlers if their nutrition improves. Very few bucks that start out as spikes stay that way throughout life. However, research does show bucks with spikes north or south seldom develop as large a rack as a buck that started out as a forkhorn or with a small basket rack that first year.

Whether or not to take spikes in the north again depends upon the manager's long-range goals for any deer herd. If you want fewer spike bucks to develop in the herd to begin with, you must either lower the deer population or increase the quality and quantity of the daily food supply.

Interestingly, some of the bucks that were fed a low-quality ration developed forked antlers even though they were nutritionally deprived. It appears that these bucks had greater genetic potential for producing large antlers despite the restraints of a low-quality diet. These same bucks continued to grow larger antlers throughout their lives than those bucks of the same age that had only spikes as yearlings. Studies focusing on bucks that appear genetically superior are just beginning as part of the continuing research.

For now, the question deals with spikes and whether or not they should be removed from the herd. To determine the genetic odds of a spike buck siring more spikes, the Kerr Area biologists selected a buck that started out with small, short spikes as a yearling. This particular animal eventually developed a 6-point rack without brow tines as a 3-year-old. This poor antler development occurred even though the buck and its offspring have been on a high-quality diet throughout their lives.

The buck was bred to numerous does. Nearly every buck born as a result of those breedings had spikes as a yearling. Very few of those bucks ever grew more than a 7-point rack—even as mature deer on excellent diets. That same line has been perpetuated for several generations and it continues to produce primarily spike yearlings that seldom develop more than a 7-point frame as mature deer.

The one exception was when the spike line herd sire was bred to one particular doe. Practically all of the bucks she gave birth to grew forked antlers as yearlings. These same bucks also grew racks much larger than the 7-points as mature animals. Even though it was previously known that a doe contributes 50 percent of a buck fawn's genetic potential, nowhere was it more dramatically demonstrated than in this instance.

In an effort to learn more about the heritability (the potential of what individuals inherit from their parents) of antler development traits, various research was conducted within the pedigreed deer herd in the Kerr Wildlife Area. Research was conducted in conjunction with Dr. John Williams, a geneticist at Texas A&M University.

Antler and Body Heritability

Below are the research results of antler and body heritability in white-tailed deer involved in the Kerr Area research.

Antler Characteristics

Number of Points:	.46
Spread:	.32
Basal circumference:	.77
Main beam length:	.54
Antler weight:	.70

Body Characteristics

Body weight:	.74

Twenty generations of known quality, age, genetic background and individually identified deer were analyzed. Such factors as body weight and antler characteristics (including: number of points, spread, basal circumference, main beam length and weight) were closely analyzed through a series of sophisticated scientific tests. (See the chart on the previous page.)

As in other research, heritability was measured from 0 to 1. The closer the number is to 1 the more heritable the trait. The closer to 0 the less heritable the trait. Based on considerable research, heritability estimates above .3 are considered practical for management (where changes can be made within the genetics of the herd or group).

As you can see in the chart, three factors rate at .70 or above, including basal circumference, antler weight and body weight. Although all factors in question are highly heritable, these three are the highest.

As a result, if you happen to own a large block of whitetail habitat or hunt in an area where you can maintain some control over the harvest of particular animals, you can use this information to decide which yearling bucks to harvest and which to pass.

Those you should allow to mature and hopefully do the breeding are those with a good number of points, relatively long main beam length and most basal circumference (in other words, those bucks that have the most massive antlers). The ones to remove are those that lack these characteristics. Spikes are the most obvious candidates. Remember, these are not "button" or "nubbin" bucks. Those terms are used to describe buck fawns—those less than 1 year old. Seldom will a 6-month-old buck fawn have more than a half inch of a chalky white antler protruding above the skin.

Say you have made the decision to shoot a spike buck in order to help improve the deer herd quality (along with harvesting does and making a conscious effort to improve the deer nutrition in your immediate area). One of the spike bucks has antlers that are 6 to 8 inches long and the other has spikes that are 3 or 4 inches long. Which do you shoot?

When I asked wildlife biologist Bill Armstrong the question, his response was, "Shoot the smaller one first and don't let the second one get away." This, of course, is where it is legal to harvest two antlered bucks on the same day of the same season.

Armstrong was also quick to point out that their research indicated antler mass was the most heritable trait and, thus, the one most important for hunters to try to preserve among the bucks in the local herd. Thus, the buck with the smaller spikes had less potential for trophy antlers. In addition it would pass on this trait to any of its offspring. Tag the smaller spike.

However, Armstrong went on to stress the importance of nutrition, harvest of both bucks and does, and habitat management in any attempt aimed at improving the quality of deer. And, most of all, it involves you. Simply shooting spikes and forgetting about the other factors will not help. You also have to be willing to harvest antlerless deer when department of wildlife biologists determine a herd has exceeded the carrying capacity of the land.

Hunters are the ultimate deer managers. You decide when to squeeze the trigger or release an arrow. Shoot spikes or let 'em walk? You've got the information. Now the decision's yours.

Antler Answers

Based on the research conducted in Texas, and now in Louisiana and other states, much has been learned about spikes. Here are some of the key conclusions reached as a result of all this research during the past 22 years:

1. Antler development is genetically based. While all white-tailed bucks have genetics to grow antlers, not all have the same genetic potential for large antlers. This potential is also determined, to some extent, by nutrition and age.

2. When spike bucks are allowed to breed does, a high percentage of the resulting bucks produce spikes as yearlings and below average antlers as mature bucks. This occurs despite good to excellent nutrition.

3. Regardless of whether a fawn is born early or late, it does not affect his genetic potential for antlers. However, those born late in the summer or early in the fall are normally deprived of excellent nutrition due to changes in vegetation.

4. Bucks with spikes as yearlings generally produce fewer points and smaller antlers in ensuing years than those that have forked antlers their first year.

5. A deer herd can be improved by removing bucks with inferior antlers and allowing those with larger antlers to do the breeding. Genetic research tells us that if traits that are highly heritable, in this case antler mass, are selected for, improvement can be seen in a relatively short period of time.

6. Bucks and does each provide 50 percent of a male offspring's genetic potential for antler development. Even though you cannot see the potential a doe provides for antler development, by carrying on a program of removing inferior antlered bucks and leaving only the bigger antlered bucks to do the breeding, genetics of does is also improved in future generations.

7. Removing spikes, even in a heavily hunted area, will not endanger the herd's breeding potential. In captive herds one buck has been know to breed as many as 40 does.

8. Periods of nutritional stress are the best time to manage for genetic improvements. Some yearling bucks produce forked racks even in a nutritionally deprived situation. This is a sure sign that these are the bucks with the best antler potential. Let 'em walk and pass on those genes.

9. The best time to tell whether a buck's antler development is inferior is when he is 1½ years old. This is when he is the easiest to age based on body characteristics, and when he is most vulnerable for harvest.

8

The Poop On Deer Pellets

by C.J. Winand

*I*t happens to every hunter at least once in his life. That uneasy feeling grips you when the deep trenches of your bowels signal you that the last bean burrito you ate the night before hasn't been sitting too well. It's a pain that hits you at about 7 a.m. in your favorite tree stand.

Since you're already 20 feet in the air, you have two options. You could climb down from your tree stand, walk to a discrete place and do your business. Or, in those really stressful situations, you could squat down over the edge of your stand (safety harness secured, of course) and wait for relief.

A problem develops if you're 20 feet in the air and you realize there isn't any toilet paper in your pocket; no way to reach all those choice leaves on the ground. Instead of panicking, you draw the trusty Gerber knife and cut off the tops of your socks. A T-shirt pocket works, too.

Been there, done that. Most every hunter has gone through something like this. In fact, my good friend, Tony Canami, is one of those guys who has left his mark in every parcel of woods in Harford County, Maryland. You always know Tony was in the woods by the number of cut-off Nike socks. Since Tony hunts almost every day, hunters in his area can tell where the hot spots are by the number of socks.

One day, Tony and I were discussing all the "science" concerning deer feces and what it can mean to hunters. Unlike the first few paragraphs, the balance of this article will focus on the art and science of deer "pelletology" from a deer biology and behavior point of view. Needless to say, this article will be full of it! Information, that is.

Many hunters are probably saying to themselves, "What can I learn from a bunch of deer droppings? Can we actually get closer to deer by learning something about deer pellets? Do all deer defecate in the same area? Are buck droppings larger than does?" Surprisingly enough, all of these questions have been answered within the scientific community.

The Tale Of The Shape

Whenever we come across a pile of droppings, the shape can give hunters many clues to what the deer have been eating. Generally,

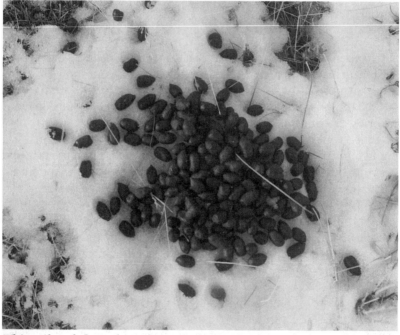

This pile of deer droppings can reveal where the local deer are feeding and where you should hunt.

round, individual droppings indicate deer are foraging primarily on leaves, browse and twigs. Whereas the pellets clumped together suggest deer have focused their attention on grasses and forbs.

Whenever you're hunting in a feeding area and see lots of lumped droppings, you should look for the closest grasses to key in on. Conversely, if a hunter identifies many round or individual droppings it would not be best to hunt a food plot with cool-season grasses.

Many hunters have tried to say they can tell the sex of the deer from the size of individual droppings. Research analyzing pellets from penned deer suggests the opposite. In fact, some of the trophy deer droppings I've observed have come from penned does. An exception occurs when you have bucks 4½ years old or older in your area. However, considering that most of the country supports high percentages of younger bucks, betting the farm that the large droppings you've found will lead you to a record-book buck wouldn't be a wise decision.

The Science Of Pelletology

Way back in 1940, researcher Logan Bennett came up with an idea that is still used in today's deer management. He found that deer defecate 13 times per day. That's right, count 'em, 13 times. It's no wonder hunters can actually smell deer! And if you're wondering if those large piles are from bucks, biologists have found that some adult bucks do, in fact, produce more pellets per group.

Biologists have also found that 75 is the average number of pellets per group. (Can you imagine the poor soul who had to count through all those samples?) So, the next time you wander onto a Boone and Crockett poop pile, you just might be a short distance "behind" a deer of a lifetime.

Another important question that deer hunters always ask biologists is, "How many deer are there in this area?" The answer, or at least a very close approximation, can be found in the number of droppings in the area. In fact, pellet counts are used by many state wildlife departments as a component to estimating deer populations.

Bennett and other biologists determined the defecation rate for deer by walking various transects along a one-square-mile area and counting every pile of "woodland nuggets." Hunters can easily do the same, and those in the North would be advised to conduct this population index every 24 hours after a snowfall. For example: If, after one day, you count 169 droppings along your transects, simply divide by 13. The density of deer within your hunting area is 13 deer per square mile. As with any population index, the more times you sample your area, the more accurate your results.

Other researchers have found that deer might average more piles of dung in the spring and fall. This is probably due to the increasing amounts of fiber added to the bulk feces between spring and fall. Evidently, as the diet changes from succulent leaves and forbs in spring to mature vegetation in summer to more coarse items in fall after leaf-drop, the number of pellet groups increase.

Other data has found that defecation rates among adult deer and juvenile deer also differ with diet. Researchers have found that bucks appear to have a higher defecation rate than does in the wintertime.

More Pellet Facts and Findings

What else can research tell us about a bunch of droppings? One very important conclusion we can reach is the approximate location that deer are feeding and bedding. Just like many people, shortly after a good meal they're off to the "reading room." Furthermore, I'll also bet the first thing you did this morning was head to the bathroom! Whenever you find a lot of deer pellets in a relatively small area, you've ventured close to one of two areas…the feeding or bedding area.

Since bedding areas are always hard to locate and you don't want to push deer from their beds, feces can be a great sign giving away a buck's bedroom.

Another field clue we can identify from pellets is the specific type of forage deer are keying on right now. With a little practice you'd be surprised at how well you can identify the different plant and mast species.

Smells Like…Pellets!

And, since you're already picking through them, I'd suggest rolling and/or rubbing around in them if it's hunting season. I better repeat this…rub them all over your hunting clothing. Before you think this is nuts, hear me out.

Did you ever wonder why a dog will roll all over a dead rabbit or opossum? Instinctively, if he can cover his predator scent with that of another prey species he will become a more efficient predator. Hunters who step in cow manure (on purpose) or roll or rub deer pellets onto their clothing and tree stand, can effectively cover some of their predator odors. Since droppings are located almost everywhere and they're free, hunters can't ask for a better cover scent.

To prove this point, I and another biologist took droppings from one deer pen and placed them on the ground of a separate pen containing different deer. The results were very interesting. The typical response included a monarch doe and her fawns coming over to investigate the strange droppings, smelling them and simply continuing on with their feeding. They did not become alarmed.

Obviously, our next test was on wild, free-ranging deer. Just like the penned deer, the wild deer checked out the unfamiliar odor, but did not become alarmed. Before conducting these tests, we hypothesized that, since penned and wild deer were able to identify other individual deer within the herd by smell, the scent of droppings from a foreign deer might cause some degree of alarm. This definitely was not the case. We also wondered what type of behavioral responses we would observe if we used urine and feces from other species.

Before we could actually test our hypothesis, I discovered an actual "feces thesis" done by researcher Howard Steinberg. Steinberg tested the response from deer encountering feces from other herbivores (vegetarians), omnivores (both vegetation and meat eaters) and carnivores (meat eaters). He found that deer had the greatest aversion toward the feces of carnivores from animals like timber wolves, dogs, bobcats and cougars. Interestingly, no matter how many times the carnivore samples were presented, the deer always exhibited alarm behavior.

Deer showed some aversion to the omnivores, but not as much as the carnivores and hardly any avoidance of feces from herbivores.

The most important finding in these studies has been that deer showed the greatest interest in the pellets from deer of separate herds. Whenever you hunt an area, it's wise to collect those special little woodland nuggets in a plastic bag and use them near your stand in a different hunting area. Since deer are generally curious animals, this technique could be the final trick you need to bag your deer. Furthermore, deer pellets keep quite well in your freezer—at least if a non-hunting family member doesn't recognize what you're storing next to the steaks.

In The End

Despite the sometimes humorous tone of this article, the science of deer pelletology should be taken seriously by whitetail hunters.

And I would venture to guess that the same behaviors would be exhibited by other ungulates like elk and other deer species. We hunters spend a lot of time analyzing the particulars of deer sign like rubs and scrapes. But there are a lot more deer pellets in the woods offering clues about deer behavior. It's time we look at this important deer sign as more than simply an indication of the "presence" of deer in the area.

If you understand how to really read all forms of deer sign, you'll be a better hunter. And that's what the science of deer hunting is all about.

9

Treeing Your Buck

by Tim Jones

*T*oo often, we hunters try to replace woodsmanship with technology. Many of us don't know the difference between a white pine and a red pine because we no longer pay attention to such things. We don't heat the cabin with wood we've cut ourselves. We don't know what plants to touch and not to touch. And as much as we might like to think we can, we can't gain all this knowledge in cyberspace.

Human nature being what it is, today's deer hunters are always looking for an easy answer. We want to know for certain that we'll absolutely get a shot at a 10-point buck by blowing a grunt call on the next-to-last day of the season during a light southeasterly breeze, a waxing moon and after dousing the area with a buck lure.

If only this deer hunting were that easy. Instead, year in and year out, it's the hunter who knows (or who pays a guide who knows) the most about deer behavior in the area being hunted who most often takes home the prize.

A big part of that equation is understanding the land we hunt— the woods, swamps and farmland fringes where the deer live. Two important features that define the world deer live in are topography (the lay of the land) and plant growth. Often the two go hand-in-hand, but in most deer hunting situations, plant growth is the more important of the two.

Plants Like Buildings

You don't have to spend much time hunting whitetails to discover that deer use the plants around them in much the same way that humans use buildings. For deer, some plant communities—trees, shrubs, forbs, grasses and crop plants are the equivalent of your local supermarket, just loaded with goodies to eat. Some plant varieties at various stages of growth are like your home, creating a comfortable place to relax and ruminate. Still other plants are like the local gym, providing the equipment needed to exercise vital muscles. Another plant community might function like your town's emergency Civil Defense shelter—a place to retreat in extremely severe weather or in the face of invasion. And, finally, other plants in the deer's world function like a singles bar—a place to pick up a willing member of the opposite sex.

The only thing deer don't have is the equivalent of offices, factories, shops or schools—their only "job" is survival. And only quick learners live.

Understanding The Relationship

Since wildlife biology emerged as a science in the 1930s, a lot of studies have been done on the relationships between white-tailed deer and the plants they need to live. Most of these works have focused on the plants that deer eat—particularly those plants that have commercial value to humans. And many northern states have studies on winter deer yards—which are created by trees of a certain age and species growing in a specific area. And, recently, some studies of rubbing and scraping behavior are taking note of the species, size and location of the trees involved.

But how much will this scientific information help a hunter? Unfortunately, none of this is absolute. Results of these studies reveal only whitetail preferences. But understanding these preferred plant species where deer are likely to feed, bed, rub and scrape can certainly stack the odds in your favor.

Let me give you an example. Last season, my two hunting partners and I were doing some quiet "pushes" on a hillside in Vermont. My assignment was to watch a certain bench on the hillside where the deer often travel. A few days earlier, a high wind had blown over two very large trees on opposite ends of that bench—one a spruce, the other a sugar maple. Those trees represented a ready source of fresh browse at a time when snow was beginning to limit feeding opportunities. I couldn't watch them both, but I knew that deer in that area relish sugar maple and eat spruce only when they're starving. So it was only a matter of time before the deer began congregating at that tree.

I chose a seat where I could cover the most likely route for escaping deer and where I could watch behind me—away from the push—for deer moving in on that downed sugar maple. I ignored the spruce, as I knew the deer would.

The push failed to move any deer. One of my partners had come through, and we were quietly waiting for the second, when I saw a fawn heading for the maple. Seconds later, a doe appeared. By the time the third deer showed, I had a solid rest and was watching through the bright Swarovski scope cranked up to 9X. With all that magnification, it was easy to see the spikes, and my Vermont rifle season ended with a touch of the trigger on my Ruger .308 Win.

Deer and Trees

As a starting point for their study of deer and trees, hunters should take advantage of any research done locally. Contact the nearest regional office of your state's wildlife agency and ask the deer biologist about studies on deer foods, winter cover or breeding behavior. A call to any nearby university with a wildlife management program can also yield information. But if that work was done more than a few miles from your hunting area, don't expect it to yield any sure-thing clues. Still, any general knowledge you take to the field with you is going to help.

To better understand the nature of the problem, take a moment to consider how adaptable whitetails really are. At the northern edges of their range, they share habitat with moose, wolves and woodland caribou—creatures adapted specifically to a climate of deep snows, bitter cold and short growing seasons. Thousands of miles south in Central America, they share swamp and tropical jungle habitat with jaguars and alligators. In between, they thrive in deep forests, farmland and suburban backyards.

In other words, the plants that are absolutely key to deer survival in one area don't even grow in others. And you don't have to travel from Minnesota to Texas to see the changes. Some years, oak trees are the key to finding deer near my home in southern New Hampshire. But where I hunt in Vermont—only a little more than 100 miles away—there's not an oak to be found.

It's been estimated that deer will feed on approximately 600 species of plants. In many instances, it's easier for the scientists to list the plants the deer won't eat than the ones they will. Also, a prime food source in one area might be totally ignored in others. In one

The fact that deer will seek out specific types of vegetation for various activities can help a hunter turn the odds in his favor, yet few take advantage of this trait.

classic study in my home state, biologists cut fresh red elder, a prime browse in the northern part of the state, and fed it to a penned herd of deer a little farther south. Even with nothing else available, the deer refused to eat it for four days!

Fortunately for hunters, however, we don't need scientists to tell us what plants are important in our hunting area. The deer will give us that information if we look. All we need is enough knowledge to be able to decipher what the deer are telling us.

Basic Biology

You might not be able to tell the difference between a hemlock and a spruce, a greenbrier and bullbrier, or a bitterbrush and willow, but the deer can! When the deer in your area show you what plant species are important to them, you can identify them by species, learn about their habitat preferences, and begin to unlock the secrets of the area you hunt.

Start with a visit to any good bookstore, especially one that specializes in nature books. A general guide such as the Golden Press *Trees of North America* will help get you started, while a regional guide to trees and shrubs and a wildflowers guide will let you sort out the rest. Carry these in your pack or vest while you're out hunting and scouting. When you see evidence of deer utilizing a specific plant, take a moment to note the species and location. It won't take long to see patterns emerge.

Plant Categories

For a hunter's purposes, it helps to identify broad categories of plants that are important to deer.

Crops: If you live in a farming area, chances are one or more of the crops in neighboring fields are helping to feed the deer. Soybeans, clover, alfalfa, corn, winter rye and a host of others are all utilized, and no hunter in farm country would think of ignoring this impact on deer behavior. Standing corn is also an often overlooked shelter for deer—they'll bed in these vast fields during summer and fall.

Forbs: For a hunter's purposes, forbs are herbaceous plants other than grasses, generally growing in open areas. In other words, weeds. Deer eat lots of 'em, and occasionally hide in 'em.

Shrubs: They're defined as low-growing, multi-stemmed, woody plants. Bushes. Again, shrubs are often a key food source and are occasionally used as cover.

Trees: They serve so many functions for deer that it's best to break them down into four sub-categories.

Mast-bearing hardwoods such as oaks, beeches, hickories, chestnuts, etc. are the big guns of the tree world for deer. Except for some agricultural crops, nothing draws deer like abundant mast. One of the few generalities that holds up from coast to coast is that deer generally prefer the sweet acorns from oaks in the white oak group (white oak, post oak, chinquapin, chestnut oak, etc.) to the more bitter, tannin-rich acorns of the red oak group (red oak, black oak, pin oak, willow oak, water oak, etc.) Fortunately, it's easy to tell which group the oak tree you're looking at is in—even without identifying the species. White oak leaves generally have rounded lobes on their leaves, while red oaks generally have pointed lobes, or at least a pointed leaf tip. You can also sample an acorn or two. The white oak acorns will taste sweet, while the red oak acorns are bitter.

A couple of other facts about most mast-bearing trees: Most white oaks produce acorns each year, while red oaks drop heavily only every other year. However, be aware that red oak acorns resist decay better than white oak acorns. So, in abundant years, they'll last far longer as a food source.

Beeches are inconsistent mast producers, but in abundant years will draw deer (and bears and turkeys) like a magnet. Beech trees are also a prime scrape location, at least in the northeast where I do most of my hunting. I think it's because the branches swoop low to within a deer's reach and are tough enough to withstand repeated chewing and rubbing. That information helped me to see (unfortunately, not shoot) the biggest buck I've ever seen.

It happened like this: I was hunting an unfamiliar area in New Brunswick, Canada, alternately rattling and moving to scout new areas. On a maple-covered hillside that showed lots of indications of deer use but no patterns, I noticed a large beech tree far up the hill. I detoured, found a huge scrape beneath this beech, and set up an ambush. The next morning, a vagrant breeze betrayed me to the buck just before he stepped clear of the last shred of cover. I got a good look at him as he leaped away. A 311-pound buck was hanging on the meat pole back at camp. This one was larger!

Other mast-bearing species such as hickories can be important. Probably the single greatest environmental catastrophe ever to face eastern wildlife was the loss of the American chestnut. It's been virtually exterminated by an imported fungus. American chestnuts annually produce abundant, highly nutritious mast.

Fruit-bearing hardwoods such as apples, cherries, persimmons and plums can provide an important food source for deer. Whitetails, of course, will feed heavily on the fruit produced by these trees, but the sweet twigs and leaves are also an attraction. In my area, it's safe to say that apples are the undoing of most deer taken by early-season hunters. In years when acorns are scarce, I've also taken a number of late-season deer that couldn't resist walking by an apple tree to see if any fruit had fallen. Also, young fruit trees, especially those that sprout along orchard boundaries, seem particularly attractive for rubbing.

The last two categories: general hardwoods like maples, birches, ashes, gums and elms; and evergreen softwoods like pines, spruces, cedars, hemlock, junipers and firs can be vitally important at times, ignored at others. These are some of the species you have to pay attention to at different times of the year to understand their importance to the local herd.

Beyond Species

For deer, the size of the tree can have as much or more impact as the species of the tree. Take, for example, the red maple. Young red maples sprouting in cut-over areas are prime deer food. When the trees mature to pole size and the branches have grown out of reach of a browsing deer, they are often rubbed by bucks—the bright white wood under the bark makes a strong visual signpost identifying a buck's presence. A mature red maple has little interest to deer, unless it falls or is cut so the top buds again are in reach for browsing.

Likewise, some young evergreens are used for food, some are preferred rub species and others are critical winter cover in deer yards. In my hunting area, hemlocks are another species that have large, low-hanging branches, and are a good bet for finding scrapes.

Burning Love

Deer have an uncanny ability to seek out and concentrate on the most nutritious food sources available to them. That's why fertilized crop fields and orchards are always such a big draw.

Because of the nutrients released in the burning process, the vegetation that grows up following a fire is always richer in protein and minerals than the vegetation in similar, unburned areas nearby. Pay close attention to burned areas from the moment the first new green appears until the last of the browse has grown out of a deer's reach.

Aye, There's The Rub

In some regions white-tailed bucks show a definite preference in the species of the trees they rub. That's the word from Grant Woods, a prominent deer researcher in South Carolina. According to Woods, while any tree of the correct size might be rubbed by a buck passing through the area, traditional rubs used by more than one buck year after year often occur on specific species with the correct "aromatic component and coloration." Thus, these species smell right and leave strong visual cues to other deer.

That's the good news. The bad news is that Woods says bucks won't go out of their way to seek out a preferred rub species. In other words, a traditional rub will occur when a tree of the correct size and species is located in a place where the deer would have been anyway. And for nontraditional rubs it's location and size of the tree, not species, that matters most.

So as you set about dissecting the deer woods in your area, remember that the pieces of information you gather are like the individual pieces of an infinite jigsaw puzzle. Eventually, if you put enough of them together, they will form a picture that is the next buck you'll harvest.

10

New Wave Whitetail Hunting

by J. Wayne Fears

*T*he hunting strategy started in Texas and swept across the South. Then it spread into the Northern and Midwestern states. Now it can be found throughout the whitetail range. No, it's not a new chain of taco restaurants. It's the new wave of whitetail hunting that stresses taking only mature bucks and a prescribed number of does. Many hunters refer to this as "trophy hunting," but white-tailed deer biologists call it "quality deer management."

This new style of deer management and hunting has actually been several decades in coming. It originated in Texas during the late '50s and early '60s when the rapid increase in deer numbers caused biologists to take a look at the management techniques—including hunting as a management tool—necessary to produce quality bucks in substantial numbers.

At the same time, there was a boom in the number of white-tailed deer hunters. Due to the scarcity of public land available for deer hunting in Texas, the demand for private hunting lands grew rapidly, popularizing the concept of leasing rights on private land for deer hunting.

White-tailed deer numbers in other Southern states were also exploding, as were the number of deer hunters. It wasn't long before leasing of private lands by groups of hunters, usually organized into hunting clubs, became widespread.

Since it had been only a few years since most of these deer populations were small or non-existent, state laws and/or club rules prohibited taking does. Often only one or two bucks could be taken by a member during a deer season. The results were rapid over-population and a declining number of large-racked bucks.

The Change To QDM

Texas deer biologists were the pioneers in developing management programs whose aim was to produce large-racked or "quality" bucks. They set harvest quotas to reduce deer numbers, including harvesting does, so that the total deer population was within the carrying capacity of the habitat. They worked with lessees and private landowners to get the buck-to-doe ratio down to 1:1, rather than the typical 1:6 or greater that an over-populated habitat usually had. They encouraged hunters to pass up small, usually immature bucks and allow the animals to live to reach 4½ years and older age classes to permit peak antler growth that's only possible with mature bucks.

The ranches that followed the biologists' advice began to produce bucks in the 150-plus Boone & Crockett point class within a few years, attracting the attention of those who were skeptical of the new program. Not only were the hunters on the ranches under quality deer management taking more large bucks, but they were getting equal enjoyment out of seeing lots of nice bucks on their property.

As this program developed, those who were hunting on leases throughout the South were enjoying taking lots of deer, but the challenge of hunting large bucks was missing; as they matured as hunters, the interest grew in taking fewer deer but higher quality bucks. This was fostered by the quality buck management success stories coming out of Texas and the growing interest in large bucks that were being shown in popular hunting magazines.

Enjoyment From Management

Many hunting club members were discovering the fun of getting involved in the deer management process. They found planting and fertilizing food plots to be a fun reason to be afield during the summer. They enjoyed learning to keep harvest records, pull jaw bones for aging, and keep accurate weights on harvested deer. As they saw how this data related to the management of the habitat and

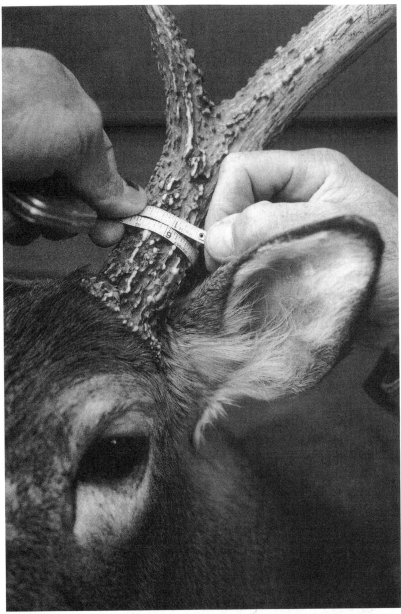

Keeping detailed records is essential for a good management program. It may seem like work, but lease partners will really get into it when they start seeing the results.

the quality of the bucks, their interest in quality deer management grew. They wanted bucks like Texas was becoming known for.

During this period, I was in charge of the wildlife division for a large paper company in Alabama. The white-tailed deer management program covered 500,000 acres, and my staff worked with some 220 hunting clubs that leased land from the company. I saw how hunters leasing land for the first time would be interested in taking any buck they saw. You must remember that Alabama has a buck-per-day bag limit. Most hunters would take several young bucks throughout the season and one or two does during the week-long either-sex season.

After two or three seasons of taking lots of small bucks and does, but never seeing a large buck on their lease, the hunters would start inquiring about how they could get into a quality buck management program. They had gotten the quest for quantity of bucks out of their system and now wanted to concentrate on quality bucks instead. The attitude was right, on many hunting club leases, to enter into a quality buck management program.

In the early 1980s, Alabama was one of the first states to use what was learned in Texas, as well as other research, to establish a deer management program that was tailored to each individual property. Under the Deer Management Assistance Program (DMP), a private landowner or lease group could elect to manage their property, under the guidance of an Alabama Game & Fish Division biologist, for the production of quality bucks.

This program, which has grown to several hundred tracts of land, requires the managers of each DMP property to keep detailed records on the weight, age, and antler size of all deer taken on the property. This is analyzed by the DMP biologist each year, and a prescribed number of doe tags are issued so that the deer population is kept below the carrying capacity of the habitat, assuring the deer of ample nutrition.

Many clubs and landowners establish a minimum antler size, such as eight points with a 14-inch spread, to assure that only mature bucks are harvested. Clubs may also require the members to take their share of the does which must be harvested each season. The results have been an increase in wall-hangers taken and a renewed challenge added to the sport. While the hunters aren't taking as many bucks, the added doe harvest assures there is no shortage of meat in the freezer.

State-aided Private Programs

The trend toward managing property for larger-racked bucks has now spread, in varying degrees, throughout the whitetail range. Several states now offer a management program for private landowners to manage their land for quality bucks, and some are implementing restrictive buck management programs on public hunting areas. Where the deer population hasn't exceeded the carrying capacity of the land, developing such a program is relatively easy; just establish minimum size and age restrictions for bucks to be harvested, and take does as needed to keep the population at a healthy level.

One county in Georgia has elected to set up such a program county-wide. Dooly County, believed to be the first county in the nation to implement such a program, is an agricultural county in south-central Georgia with proven genetics for producing large-antlered bucks. Four bucks from that county are listed in the Boone & Crockett record book. Dooly County's deer population is considerably less than the carrying capacity, making it a good test sight for a trophy program. Perhaps most important, the citizens voted to impose the new regulations that would restrict the size bucks that could be taken.

The county completed its first deer season under the new county-wide regulations, which include a minimum outside spread of 15 inches on all bucks taken. In that area, that's roughly ear tip to ear tip, making it easy to field-judge legal bucks. There is no minimum on number of points. The season bag limit is five deer, three of which must be antlerless. All deer harvested must be taken to a check station.

It is felt by the biologist in charge of the program that a 15-inch outside spread limit would protect all 1½-year-old bucks and 35 percent of 2½-year-old bucks. Bucks in that area reach "trophy" proportions in about four years, and this antler size restriction would permit a large percentage of the bucks to reach that age class.

This three-year research project will be watched throughout the country to see if the county can achieve their goals. Biologists are quick to caution that even if this project is successful, it may not be for every county. Many counties do not have the genetics and nutrition to have a management program like Dooly County. Each county must be evaluated based on its own merits.

Perhaps the most valuable product of these changes in deer management is the quality buck hunter. He is more willing to spend hours on a cold stand and pass up bucks that, in the past, he would have taken without hesitation. He is willing to learn the skills to locate mature bucks, field judge them to assure they reach the specified minimums, and take them with one well-placed shot. He is a hunter who would rather take one really nice buck than several smaller, immature bucks.

The quality buck hunter understands the role of harvesting does in the management plan and is willing to take his share of these animals. This is a hunter who finds deer management interesting and gets involved in habitat improvement, harvest data record-keeping and setting clear rules that maintain a quality deer population.

There is no doubt we will see an increase in the number of quality buck hunters, hunting leases and private and public lands in quality deer management programs. The new wave of deer hunting will result in more trophy-class bucks than we could have ever imagined, and many areas that rarely, if ever, produced an above-average buck may see many such animals in the future.

What Makes A Big Buck

Age. Of all the factors affecting antler development, age is probably the easiest to understand and, with cooperation from all hunters on a tract of land, control. Simply put, a buck must live long enough to develop a large set of antlers. During the first three or four years of a buck's life, his body has priority over antlers as far as the use of nutrients is concerned. If the food quality available to the buck is low, then the vast majority of the nutrients are going into the sustenance of the buck's body rather than to the development of large antlers.

After the fourth year, more nutrients in healthy, well-fed bucks go into the development of antlers, and maximum antler growth occurs during the 5½- to 7½-year-old period of a buck's life. In many areas where hunting pressure is heavy or where hunters don't appreciate trophy-class bucks, very few bucks live longer than 2½ years; consequently, few trophy animals are seen in that area. I have seen heavily-hunted public hunting areas and hunting leases where few bucks lived to be 2½ years of age. Only a dreamer would hunt in these areas for a trophy buck.

Nutrition. Nutrition is a more complex factor in antler development and relates to two areas—amount of food and quality of the food available.

The amount of food available is influenced greatly by the number of deer on a specific tract of land. From the river bottoms of Idaho to the swamps of Louisiana, deer habitat can produce only a certain amount of high-quality deer food per acre, and this can sustain only a limited number of deer in a healthy condition. The number that can be provided for by the habitat is known as the "carrying capacity" of that habitat.

If there are fewer deer in the habitat than available food, the herd will usually be in excellent condition because all deer are well-fed. When the carrying capacity is reached or exceeded, the habitat is considered over-populated. That same amount of food must be shared by more deer, and on the average, they will not be adequately nourished. Thus, bucks will have small antlers.

The quality of the food available to bucks is usually determined by the soil types found in an area and whether or not the area is over-browsed by deer and/or livestock. In areas where there are fertilized agricultural crops, deer have a ready source of highly nutritious food, often to the regret of the farmer. In a growing number of areas, wildlife managers, landowners, and hunting lease managers are learning how to fertilize native plants, such as honeysuckle, in order to offer deer top-quality food.

Genetics. While genetics plays an important role in producing bucks with exceptional antlers, it is one of the factors that land managers in most parts of the country can do little about. Stocking bucks with big antlers into a deer population with bucks growing small antlers does little to overcome the problem. It's far better to work on other solutions such as habitat improvement or population control.

Scientific Deer Hunting Strategies

1

Feed, Scrapes and Stands: The Keys To All-Season Success

by J. Wayne Fears

Being consistently successful in your pursuit of trophy white-tailed bucks requires that you be well-versed in deer habits and habitat preferences from the first day of bow season through the last day of the last muzzleloader season. In fact, you really need to understand the whole year of the whitetail if you want to boost your odds of taking a big buck in the fall.

However, during the hunting season in most any part of the country, there are three primary keys to "locking on" to big bucks. They are feed, scrapes and stands, and each applies directly to a different part of the season.

Feed

Throughout the whitetail range, there are many hunting seasons that open and close before the rut ever gets underway. Some of these are special seasons, such as for bow or muzzleloading firearms, and in some cases, an area's entire deer hunting season may occur before the rut begins.

What this means to NAHC members is that hunting techniques based on the rut won't get the job done. It's hard to hunt scrapes when there aren't any! The pre-rut hunter won't get any action if he douses himself with sex or attractant lures. Hunting whitetails before the rut is a different game requiring a different game plan.

Pre-rut hunting is really a matter of catching old mossy horns on the way to or from the dinner table, or better yet, at the dinner table. The pre-rut hunter must know the deer's preference for food in the particular area he plans on hunting, and he must have the skills to recognize these foods when scouting and hunting.

There are a number of resource people available to hunters who can help in learning the field plants of preference to deer in a local area. Extension service county agents, soil conservation service agents, conservation officers, wildlife biologists, game management area managers and forest rangers are just a few of the people who can help teach you the plants deer prefer to eat during the early fall in your hunting area.

During my career as a wildlife biologist, I have seen a lot of hunters who couldn't tell a white oak tree from an elm and were too shy to ask for help. I would rather ask for help than waste my time sitting watching an elm, waiting for a buck to come feed on its acorns!

Year round, the white-tailed deer's diet is limited to what is available within the travel range of that particular animal. He may eat practically any type of vegetation at one time or another. Deer, once thought to be primarily browsers, consume large quantities of fruits, mushrooms, acorns, nuts and herbaceous material, such as grasses and weeds.

Since deer feed on whatever is available, what they eat changes from season to season. Green browse and herbage are their main spring and summer foods. As fall approaches, the deer will switch to falling mast, such as beechnuts, acorns, soft-shelled hickory nuts, and even pecans. If it is a fall during which the mast crop is poor, evergreen browse such as honeysuckle and smilax (greenbrier) is important to the whitetail.

During the winter, deer in many areas, especially the snow belt, cease to have preference in foods. During these trying days, it's what's available that counts. If agricultural crops are available, they are eaten. If little else is available, then pine seedlings and other less nourishing foods are eaten.

Since pre-rut hunters are the most interested in knowing deer foods during the early fall, let's look at each deer food group and see what the deer will most likely be feeding on. Please remember it would require an entire book to cover all pre-rut foods. These are just some of the major foods found in whitetail country to serve as a guide.

Perhaps the most important foods to deer during the fall are fruits and nuts. Wild persimmon, palmetto berries, apples, wild grapes, white oak acorns, beechnuts, hawthorn fruit, and dogwood berries are just a few fruits and nuts found in the whitetail range. Of these, deer seem to relish acorns above the others.

Acorns, although low in protein, are high in carbohydrates. In years when acorns are plentiful, deer fatten quickly in the fall and reproduce well in the next year. Only a small percentage of acorns ripen to maturity. Drought may speed up the acorn drop; however, the acorn drop usually occurs in late September through October and November depending on what part of the country you hunt it. Most acorns are eaten soon after they drop to the ground, but a few, especially from red oaks, may be available until spring.

Of the two groups of oaks, white and red, deer seem to have a high preference for white oaks. I have seen deer walk through very heavy drops of red oak acorns to get to a white oak tree that was dropping acorns. Most deer managers believe this occurs because the white oak acorn is much sweeter and usually larger than the red oak acorn. Many hunters have found that a tree stand in a grove of white oaks during good mast years is a very productive place to be.

Most hunters are aware of the deer's preference for white oak acorns; however, many hunters can't identify the white oak tree, especially after the leaves fall off - that is, during hunting season. Here, in general, is an easy way to tell the difference between red oaks and white oaks.

Red Oak. Leaves have pointed lobes that are tipped with bristles or spines. Acorns are found on second year growth and do not mature until the finish of the second growing season. Also, they are bitter and the inside of the shell is hairy. Bark is dark and furrowed.

White Oak. Leaves have rounded, smooth lobes. Acorns are found on new growth and mature in one growing season. Also, they are comparatively sweet and the inner surface of the shell is smooth. The bark is gray to almost white and is scaly, often looking similar to a hickory.

Deer enjoy leaves and twigs of many woody plants. Plants such as Japanese honeysuckle, greenbrier, strawberry bush, red maple, sassafras, wild rose, yellow poplar, blackberry, morning glory, alder, sourwood, wild cherry and persimmon are only a small sample of browse preferred by deer. A few seasons back, at my hunting lodges, we had a total failure of mast in our oak trees. There were no acorns to be found. However, the honeysuckle and greenbrier grew thick and lush due to a wet summer and a warm fall. Our hunters hunted in stands along thickets of these two plants and took some of the fattest deer I've ever dressed.

Nonwoody plants, or herbage as they are sometimes called, are considered deer foods, but not to an extent to be an advantage to hunters. Most broadleafed herbaceous species are likely to be utilized by deer. Grasses and hedges are eaten in limited amounts, as are bracken and other species of fern. Often these type plants emerge in profusion following a forest or range fire. Some of the best pre-rut deer hunting I've found has been in one-year-old burn areas where herbage plants were abundant.

Many farm crops attract heavy deer feeding—winter wheat, peas, alfalfa, sweet potatoes, soybeans, and corn, to name a few. Agricultural crops are especially important after acorns are consumed. Damage may reach the point that certain crops cannot be produced in the presence of deer populations.

Fertilization and irrigation make crops especially attractive. Winter greens such as alfalfa, wheat, oats, rye grass, and covers usually attract heavy deer usage.

Deer feed in a much different pattern than many hunters think. It is common belief that they feed only in the early morning hours and the late afternoon hours. While this is a general pattern, there is much more to it than that, and the pre-rut can take advantage of these little known traits.

When the hunting pressure is on during the hunting season, deer will stay hidden during the daylight hours and feed during the night. On bright, moonlit nights, it has been my experience to see deer feed at night and move very little during the day. In these two situations, the pre-rut hunter will find that late afternoon stalks or stands will be productive in the vicinity of the feeding areas.

Deer have a way of knowing when bad weather or a cold front is on the way. Some 12 to 24 hours before the weather hits their area, they will feed heavily, often feeding all day. When the storm hits, they will bed down and wait it out for as long as several days. Then when the weather breaks, they will move again and catch up on their eating. These two periods offer the pre-rut hunter an excellent opportunity to catch ol' mossy horns at the table.

It is also worthy of mention that when food is scarce, deer will feed longer, simply because it takes longer to get the amount of food their body requires.

Tactics for hunting feeding deer are limited only by the hunter's

Agricultural crops are especially important to whitetails after mast like acorn and apples are gone.

ingenuity. A number of successful hunters like to hunt trails leading from food sources, such as mast-producing oaks or alfalfa fields, to thick bedding areas. Across trails which appear to be used, they tie a black thread at a height of about three feet (to prevent coyotes, dogs, etc., from breaking it). By checking the thread often during the day, they can tell about when the trail is being used.

A lot of hunters in farm country hunt along the edges of farm crops such as soybeans, corn, oats, rye, and wheat. While these crops attract deer, too often hunters take a stand in the edge of the field hoping to see a deer out in the field. What I have learned by hunting around the fields on my hunting lands is that deer, particularly pre-rut bucks, will often mill around in the woods adjacent to the fields for a period of time before venturing into the field. By scouting fields, some 20 to 60 yards back in the cover where their trails can be observed, deer, especially older bucks, may be seen an hour or more before they intend to go into the field.

When hunting prior to the rut, leave the sex lure or scent at home. Use a cover scent that best matches a scent the deer are familiar with. Use pine scent if you hunt in the piney woods, acorn scent around oaks, fox scent if there are a lot of fox in the area. The point is to use something the deer are accustomed to smelling.

One of the toughest jobs when scouting for feeding areas is deciding which area to hunt. Many hunters select an area which has either some mast-producing trees, agricultural crops, lots of deer tracks, or deer droppings, or simply looks good. However, as is often the case, this is not enough, especially during the years when there is a lot of food available to deer.

A friend of mine taught me a good technique for scouting the pre-rut season. He spends a lot to time seeking out areas which have preferred deer food readily available. I have seen him spend days looking for just the right spot, which for him is a feeding area, such as under a white oak tree, where there is plenty of food and lots of deer droppings.

His trick is to find droppings of three different ages. He likes to discover some that are shiny, damp and very black. These are only a few hours old. Then he wants to see some that are dry, but still somewhat shiny. These will be about two days old. Then he will look for some that are dull in color and may be falling apart. They are several days old. His theory is that finding a lot of droppings of varying age is a good indication that deer are feeding that area on a regular basis.

There must be something to his theory. I've seen it work many times for him, and it's now working for me, too.

Pre-rut hunting can be very productive if you understand the deer's menu. In many areas, pre-rut hunting means you get to hunt ahead of the mass of hunting pressure and the bucks are going about their routine in a normal fashion. It's a great time to be hunting.

Scrapes

After sitting in a cold tree for a whole morning watching two scraped-out spots on an old logging road 30 yards away, I felt I might be the victim of a practical joke. I certainly had never heard of hunting white-tailed bucks in such a fashion.

As time passed, I started daydreaming about the events that led me here. I had recently moved to south Georgia to run a wildlife management program for the University of Georgia. When deer season opened, I took off a few days to try my hand at killing a buck in the flat, pine-palmetto woods west of the Okefenokee Swamp. I had enjoyed many successful deer hunts in the Appalachian Mountains, so I thought the same hunting methods would work down here.

How wrong could I be? After several days without even seeing a deer, I was ready to give up.

J. Lee Rentz, then manager of the Suwannoochee Wildlife Management Area, recognized that I was having trouble hunting this swampy terrain. "Get into my truck," he told me. "I'm going to teach you how to hunt deer." I knew he had spent many years working with whitetails, so I welcomed the opportunity.

"The most predictable thing we know about white-tailed bucks is that they are unpredictable," J. Lee began. "I only know of one thing that bucks do consistently enough for hunters to rely on, and that's work scrapes. I'm sure they didn't teach you college boys about scrapes in school, but no matter where you find white-tailed bucks, they work scrapes."

We continued riding until we came to the edge a recent clear-cut. Leaving the truck, we started walking along the edge, where the clear-cut and the adjacent woods met. We immediately started finding fresh rubs on small samplings growing next to the woods. Suddenly, J. Lee stopped. Pointing at a scraped-out spot about two feet in diameter, he told me to pick up a handful of the sandy soil and smell it.

Stepping down, I grabbed some of the dirt; it had the strong smell of urine.

"Now look up," he instructed.

I did and saw where the overhanging bushes were broken and shredded about four feet above the scrape.

"This is a sure sign of a mature buck," J. Lee continued. "If you follow the edge of this clear-cut, you will probably find several more scrapes. When a buck is in the peak of his rut, he will stake out his territory by arbitrarily making scrapes. Then, he will check his scrapes to see if an interested doe has been by, and to see if another buck has entered his territory."

"How will he know?" I asked.

"The visiting deer will usually paw the scrape and urinate on it," J. Lee responded. "If there isn't a doe hanging around or a rival buck spoiling for a fight, the home buck will freshen his scrape by urinating in it and chewing the overhanging branches. Also, he will probably rub his antlers on nearby saplings. Now, all you have to do is sprinkle a few drops of urine-based deer lure in the scrape, then move to one side where the wind won't blow your scent to the scrape. Find a good hiding spot and wait for old mossy horns to stagger in."

Suddenly I was startled from my daydream by a grunting sound coming from the logging road. Since there were wild hogs in the area, I was sure it was an old boar coming to root around in my carefully-selected scrape. I caught a movement off to my right, and slowly turning, saw a six-point buck boldly walking down the road. He was heading for the scrape. I couldn't believe it!

This buck was breaking all the rules. He was moving during the middle of the day, he wasn't using any caution, and he wasn't being quiet. He approached the scrape stiff-legged with his nose held high. As I eased my .30-06 into shooting position, I knew I was not the victim of a joke, but rather the very fortunate student of a dependable way to hunt whitetails.

Many years have passed since my introduction to scrape hunting. I have spent each season since trying to perfect this method of hunting. Fortunately, I've received some expert help along the way. Some of the most interesting information was provided by Francis X. Lueth, one of the nation's foremost whitetail biologists. Francis has worked with white-tailed deer for 40 years. He retired from the Alabama Game and Fish Division after 30 years of whitetail research to become a deer management consultant.

When asked about whitetail scrapes, he quickly pointed out that he was giving me only his opinion based on his observations and research. Different biologists have different opinions about this phenomenon.

For someone to be a good scrape hunter, Francis began, he should understand the rut. The rut, he said, is an evolutionary thing that has been worked out over hundreds of years so fawns will be weaned at the same time the mast falls. Because of this and several other reasons, the rut varies from area to area in any given state.

The hunter should also know something about rubs. There are two kinds. The first, which occurs during late summer or early fall, is by bucks rubbing velvet off their new antlers. The second type is during the peak of the rut, at the same time bucks are making scrapes. These rubs are probably used to mark the buck's territory. Apparently the buck leaves his scent by rubbing a gland found near the eye.

Scrapes are made mostly by dominant bucks that are 2½ years or older. This is just what the trophy hunter likes to hear! Most scrapes are made on the fringes of the buck's territory, and more often than not, will be at the base of a bush.

I asked Francis if a buck had a set number of scrapes or if they have any particular configuration. The answer was no, to both questions. "Sometimes, you may find several in a row along a logging road, and again, you may find only one or two on a ridge. But there is no known pattern."

The buck works his scrapes for periods of up to 30 days. However, this may vary, depending on the availability of does, man's intrusion, etc.

To learn more about scrape hunting and to obtain more opinions from wildlife biologists, I surveyed 35 wildlife agencies throughout the whitetail range. I obtained answers from Saskatchewan to Florida, receiving a variety of responses to the following:

1. The dates of their whitetail season;
2. Estimated date of the peak of the rut;
3. Did the rutting dates vary in their area;
4. Were scrapes made by rutting bucks;
5. Did anyone hunt scrapes; and
6. In their opinion, does it pay to hunt scrapes.

The results were interesting. The peak of the rut in most areas occurred during November. In many states, it peaked during the archery season. In almost half of the states, the rutting period varied throughout the state. As to why the rutting date varied, the biologists were not consistent in their opinions. Many indicated temperature changes, hormonal activity triggered by varying sunlight, heredity, diet and north-south latitude variation. Many said the peak varied from year to year in the same region, because of changes in population, available food, weather, etc.

Almost all of the biologists agreed that white-tailed bucks made scrapes. Two replies from the Plains states questioned how much scrape hunting was actually done in their states. Most said there was little scrape hunting in their area and eight said they knew of no one who used the technique!

Perhaps the most important information obtained from the survey were the results from the last question: "Do you think scrape hunting would pay off in your area?" Only three biologists said no, and again these were from Plains states. But 28 of the biologists replied with a firm yes, while five indicated yes under varying circumstances.

The actual scrape hunting technique is quite simple. Let's take it from the top.

1. During the summer, select your hunting area. Locate a biologist who is either responsible for that area or familiar with it. Ask him the probable date of the rut and when it will peak. This will be the best time to hunt scrapes.

2. Once you know when the rut is likely to occur, find out which type of hunting is allowed during that period. You may have to pick up your bow or muzzleloader to hunt during the rut.

3. While waiting for the hunting season, find a source of buck lure made up primarily of urine. Your sporting goods dealer can help you.

4. As the rutting season approaches, begin to scout your hunting area. Look for rubs on saplings or small trees, and for scrapes. Don't let earlier rubs fool you. The early rubs are usually in more secluded thickets and will be obviously old. Try to find rubs that are fresh and in more open areas, often near scrapes.

5. Determine that the scrape is fresh. Has the dirt been disturbed recently? Does the soil have a strong urine odor? Have the overhanging bushes been chewed? Are there fresh rubs in the area? If the answer to these questions is yes, you are on a hot one! Be cautious. Leave as little human scent as possible. Try putting urine deer lure on your boots and trouser cuffs to cover up your scent.

6. Check out the surrounding area for more scrapes. In the case of a field edge, logging road, or ridge top, walk along the feature for several hundred yards. The ideal setup is to get where you can see several scrapes from one position. More than once I have seen bucks' territories overlap, with each animal having scrapes in the same area. If you find one of these places, you're all set for the hunt of a lifetime.

7. Once you have found a group of scrapes, select several possible blinds, because in the morning, the wind may be blowing in a different direction. Make sure you can see all around each scrape. Nothing is more frustrating than to be in a fallen treetop watching a scrape and when the buck arrives, find that branches prevent you from seeing more than its hind quarter.

8. On the day of the hunt, squirt a few drops of deer lure in the scrape. Then soak a small piece of flannel cloth in urine deer lure and hang it on a bush near a fresh scrape. The cloth should be about five feet off the ground.

9. Arrive before daylight and stay until after sunset. Remain observant throughout the day. Remember, a buck in rut feeds very little and breaks the early-morning, late-afternoon movement patterns. He is likely to show up at any time. Also listen for any unusual sounds. You may hear a buck before you see him.

10. Plan on spending at least three days watching the scrapes.

As with most techniques, scrape hunting demands patience, but when you know there is a buck in the area and the he'll be back, patience is a lot easier to come by.

Stands

Hunters have long debated the attributes of hunting from a stand as opposed to stalking. However, a situation that occurred while I was preparing this piece reminded me of just how valuable stand hunting can be to the hunter.

I was guiding a group of hunters out of my Stagshead Lodge in west-central Alabama. One morning, a hunter asked if he could stalk hunt a long creek bottom that has typically been home for several bucks. I agreed with him that a slow stalk hunt could be very productive.

The next morning, he was in the creek bottom long before daylight. He hunted the entire area until about noon without seeing a deer, but he did find a great deal of sign.

Three mornings later, a new hunter asked to work the same area. He was an experienced hunter, so I felt his odds were good for producing a fine buck. At noon, when I drove my four-wheel-drive to the bridge to pick him up, he was wearing a wide grin on his face. At his feet was a handsome buck of generous proportions. The hunter enthusiastically related his success story.

Shortly after daylight, he had spotted an old permanent stand in a birch tree. Recognizing that the vegetation was thick along the creek, he decided to spend the morning in the tree stand. He had been there for less than an hour when the heavy forkhorn came through the thicket. The rest of the story was lying at his feet.

A few mornings later, a third hunter requested to stalk hunt the same area. When I picked him up, he was empty-handed. He had jumped several bucks, but the creek bottom was so thick that all he could see were the flags of escaping deer.

Two days passed and no one hunted the area. Finally, a fourth hunter approached me. Again, this was an experienced hunter who I felt could put down a nice buck. When I picked him up at the bridge, his story was the same as the second hunter. He hollered very excitedly, "Fears, I'd sure appreciate it if you'd go back up there to an old tree stand I found and help me drag out a five-pointer." This hunter had spotted the same tree stand early in the morning and from it, had shot the animal.

The lesson we can learn from these experiences is that stand hunting has a definite place in deer hunting. And, in many instances, can be more effective than stalk hunting.

The first step in learning how to stand hunt is knowing how to pick a location. Far too many hunters walk a short distance into the woods, pick the first tree that looks any good and set up their stand. By noon, they're wondering why they haven't seen a deer. Stand hunting is simple, but not that simple.

To see deer, you must get to an area that has whitetails and where the odds are in your favor.

If possible, spend as much time scouting as you can before the season opens. Get to know the terrain as well as you know your back yard. Once you get a feel for the lay of the land, start to collect all the information you can about deer habitat. Spend some time talking with a biologist or other conservation official who knows the area.

Once you've collected your information, return to the hunting spot a week before the season. Deer movements and feeding habits change with the season and the food supply, so it's unwise to look for stand sites too early.

An example is a situation where a hunter scouted an area in August. The deer were moving into the creek bottoms to feed on the honeysuckle. He selected a stand accordingly. When he returned in November, he didn't see a deer because they were feeding on white oak acorns along the ridges.

On this final scouting trip, be systematic in locating your stands. Don't make the mistake many stand hunters make—selecting the first stand they find that enables them to look out over a large territory.

Begin your scouting by locating food plants. Keep a record on your topo map. Once you find an ample supply of food, look for tracks and fresh droppings. If there is a lot of sign and the food supply is abundant, you may want to consider a stand in or near the feeding site. Many successful stand hunters set up only in areas with choice deer food, like groves of white oak that have dropped a large supply of acorns.

Next, look for trails leading to these feeding areas. These well-worn trails often connect one food supply with another, but more they lead from feeding areas to bedding sites. In hill country, bucks like to bed down on brushy slopes, usually near the heads of creeks or ravines. In flat country, they prefer thick creek bottoms. From these secluded areas, they move each day and/or night to the food source.

Record the trails on your map. If you find a heavily-used trail, you may want to consider a stand along the route.

You may find a spot where several trails come together. It may be a choice feeding area, a low saddle between two steep ridges, or at a stream crossing. If you find such an intersection and there is ample sign like fresh droppings, tracks or slides (where deer have slid down a stream bank), you have found an excellent location for a stand. Deer movement is often concentrated at an intersection, so you have a good change of seeing more than one animal.

Your basic scouting is complete once you have selected one or more stand sites. But before you return home, revisit the site you plan to use on opening morning. Select several spots, or if you use a portable tree stand, several trees. Remember, you will be returning in the dark, yet you must be able to ding each site quickly and with as little effort as possible. The wind may be blowing away form almost any direction on opening morning, forcing you to switch to another stand. The only thing more frustrating than to be on stand at daylight and find that the wind is carrying your scent toward the deer trail, is not having an alternative-plan site in mind.

As you select your alternate sites, think of the various ways the wind might blow, the direction of the sun at sunrise and your field of view. It is better to break sticks out of your stand on a scouting trip than on opening morning.

Another point to remember is to avoid stands on ridge tops. There, you would be silhouetted against the sky and your every movement would be easily seen by deer. Put yourself in the place of a deer and evaluate your stands. This will help you locate your spots where you will become a part of the woods and not a strange object to be avoided. Make use of fallen trees and thickets. It is always good to have a tree to your back, both for comfort and to break up your lines.

Often in my deer hunting seminars, novice hunters ask why it is advantageous to hunt from a tree stand. My answer usually turns into a two or three hour lecture. Tree stands offer a number of definite advantages over ground blinds. First, the hunter's scent remains above the animal or in a small area surrounding his stand. Being cautious of the wind direction and wearing a cover scent assures you of seeing more game.

Another benefit is concealment. Many deer will pass near the tree stand and never look at the human mass perched above their eye level. Occasionally a deer might look up and spot the hunter, especially if he does not remain still. However, the conscientious hunter who places his tree stand some 12 to 20 feet about the ground has a decided advantage over any deer that walk by. Be aware that some states have height limits for placing man-made tree stands. Also, tree stands may not be allowed on some lands owned by timber companies.

If legal, situating your tree stand high above ground affords a good view of the surrounding area. Where the cover is extremely thick, such as creek with cane bottoms, swamps with lots of alder and willow, dense palmetto, groups of conifers, and other areas that would be almost impossible to hunt from the ground, the hunter in a portable tree stand can select a well-positioned tree, then look down into the cover.

The elevated stand also gives the hunter an opportunity to observe unspooked deer, enabling him to make a clean kill. This is important to those who enjoy tasty venison. The majority of animals taken from a tree stand do not see the hunter and are unalarmed. This assures the hunter of getting a good shot at an animal that is moving slowly.

Being perched on a tree stand does restrict your movement, which can be to your advantage. The hunter who has little room in which to twitch and move has less chance of being noticed by deer. The ground hunter who is stretching, sitting down, standing up, and walking around often reveals his location long before he ever sees the animals.

The tree stand instills patience in many hunters who normally lack it, and that may be one of the most important keys to killing big bucks. Once you have gone to the trouble of erecting your stand, climbing up the tree and getting situated, you are more likely to stay put for a long periods than someone who is free to move about on the ground. This alone has forced many hunters to exercise patience, resulting in more success.

Some of the disadvantages of tree stand hunting are quite obvious. Putting up a portable tree stand can make a lot of noise. You may, in fact, startle deer in the immediate area for a short time. However, it has been my experience that whitetails do not stay frightened for long, nor do they move very far way. Several times I have barely climbed into my tree stand, attached my safety belt and sat down when a deer suddenly appeared within bow range. This has led me to believe that the animal was nearby and my sounds did not bother him at all. In fact, it may have been attracted by the noise—remember, deer are very curious critters.

Another disadvantage of tree stands is that they can be extremely cold places to hunt on frigid days. However, you can overcome the cold by wearing clothing that is designed for hunting in winter. Dress to be warm. If you are unbearably cold, you will find it impossible to remain still for any length of time.,

Many hunters complain about toting a heavy tree stand into the woods. Granted, a 20- to 30-pound portable stand can be a chore to carry. To overcome the problem, I try to be very thorough while scouting, pinpointing the spot where I want my stand, then selecting the most direct route to the area. I often hunt on private land where I know that few, if any, other hunters will be around. In this instance, I leave my stand on the tree for the duration of the hunt. I tried this on a public hunting areas, but once had a tree stand stolen, even though I locked it to the tree. Be sure to check on the legality of leaving your stand in the woods.

Selecting a good tree for stand hunting is not always easy. First, do not use one that is leaning, crooked, dead or one that has low limbs or a large base, such as a cypress. Choosing the wrong tree can cause problems.

Years ago, I was guiding a hunter who had just purchased a new tree stand. I showed him an area with several bucks and turned him loose. Late that afternoon I saw him waving from a road in the area. When I got to the hunter, he looked like he had been in a fight with a bear. He had selected a cypress tree for his tree stand, not noticing that the higher he climbed the smaller the trunk became. He got up to 30 feet where the tree was too small for the adjustment he had made on the large tree butt. The stand broke out and he slid down the tree, hugging it all the way. Had he picked a tree with more uniform diameter, he would not have had this problem.

Another factor to consider is your background. Walk around and look where deer are likely to appear, then look at where you will be in the tree. Will you stick out against the sky like a sore thumb, or will you blend in with green, brown, or gray vegetation in the background? I prefer hunting from trees that have some foliage to hide me, but without limbs and branches that block my gun swing.

When selecting a tree, it is wise to bring your stand so you can put it into the tree. Take a small hand axe or saw for trimming branches. Study the position you will be in on opening day. Can you move in the direction you like? Can you see as much as you like? Take your time; choosing the right tree can be critical to your success of failure.

Many hunters wait until the morning of the hunt to try out a new tree stand. Some even carry their stands in the original packing cartons, then are shocked to find they have to assemble the stand. Many stands require 30 to 40 minutes to assemble. It is better to put it together at home. Be sure to take all of the squeaks and noises out of the stand. Practice putting it up in a tree in your backyard or at a nearby woods. Learn how to safely take your firearm up into the stand without damaging the gun. This practice will give you the confidence necessary to be a successful hunter.

Always carry a day pack with you with enough essentials to allow you to stay a full day on the tree stand. The majority of large bucks are taken between 9 a.m. and 3 p.m. Many stand hunters become bored, tired, cold or impatient about mid-morning, then leave their stands to stretch their muscles or to head back to camp or their vehicles. They don't return to their tree stands until late afternoon, then hunt until dark.

The hunter with a day pack loaded with provisions can remain on the stand all day. This gives him an opportunity to spot those large bucks that tend to move when many hunters are absent from the woods.

In your day pack, carry such items as food, hot drink, a first-aid kit, empty containers for urination to save trips down the tree, extra clothing and ammunition and survival gear. There are many other items, depending on the needs of each hunter, that can be carried.

You can attach the day pack to your stand and carry it up as you climb, or tie it to a rope and lift it up into the tree along with your gun or bow.

Another important item is binoculars. With my binoculars, I have spotted many deer that, in years gone by, I would have overlooked. Binoculars can be especially helpful during the rifle season. A tree stand that has been properly placed may provide shots up to 200 yards.

A camouflage face mask such as the type used by turkey hunters is also a good idea. I have heard many hunters say that when deer looked at them, the animals always stared into their eyes. What these hunters failed to recognize is that their white faces, not their eyes, were the most visible parts of their bodies. A camouflage mask will make you less visible, but not restrict your vision. White hands can also give away the hunter; camouflage gloves will correct that problem.

Many stand hunters wear snowmobile suits and insulted boots. They keep their clothing loose, so it does not restrict circulation to their hands and feet. Much of their clothing is wool and they wear such things as Balaclava-type hats, which are extremely warm and may be worn either as a hat or rolled down to cover the face and neck, much like a ski mask.

Be sure to bring along several elastic shock cords of varying lengths. Shock cords with an S-hook on each end can be used to hang such things as your coat, day pack, lunch or whatever.

Perhaps the most important item is a safety belt. Not only does it keep you from falling, it will also steady your aim, especially when shooting a rifle or muzzleloader at deer some distance away. A properly adjusted safety belt can make the entire day go a lot smoother, because it eliminates the fear of falling.

Since a buck has his nose tuned in at all times for unfamiliar odors, the stand hunter would be wise to avoid smoking and packing strong-smelling food in his lunch. Along the same lines, if nature calls, leave your stand and travel a good distance downwind before answering the call. Or use a bottle that can be tightly capped. Keep your stand area as odor-free as possible.

When you arrive at your stand on opening morning, first check the wind. Select the stand that is downwind from your watching area. Get comfortable before daylight. As the new day dawns, be still and alert. Remember that as long as a deer doesn't smell you or see you move, he will follow his usual route. Use your ears and listen for any sounds that might reveal the presence of deer.

It bears repeating that the stand hunter must be patient. Don't give up just because you failed to see a deer on your first day. If you researched your stand site and if you found ample sign, then you are probably in a good area. Maybe the deer fed during the night or maybe the sudden influx of hunters caused them to stay bedded. Remain on your stand for at least three days before you consider changing locations.

The stand hunter who penetrates the back country, thinks like a deer, and watches the wind, will enjoy venison every year of his hunting career.

2

Making Sense Of Deer Scents

by Gary Clancy

Nobody I knew 25 years ago used deer scent to improve his odds of bagging a whitetail, but when I plunked down a buck-fifty for the first bottle of deer urine I ever saw, I had high hopes.

I spotted it on the counter while selling muskrat hides to the local fur buyer. Three days into the buck season, I still hadn't the courage to use it. Hey, if it didn't work, I didn't want the guys laughing at the kid in camp for falling for some slickster's gimmick, but I was desperate. Four bucks hung on the meat pole behind the old cabin; none of them were mine.

So, on that cold November morning, I cracked the cap and poured some of the juice onto the toes of my pac boots. About every 100 steps, I dumped a few more drops. It wasn't pretty, but it's probably the way most deer hunters begin experimenting with deer scents. By the time I got to my stand and went to wipe my nose with the back of my glove, I wondered if more stink was on my hand than on my boots.

The first hour that morning was uneventful, just a couple of shots off in the distance. I was about ready to search out a better spot when I heard a buck grunting. The buck's rapid approach grew louder and he was grunting with every breath. I pulled the old pump 12 gauge into position just as the buck—a 7-pointer with a couple of busted tines—hurried over the ridge. He had his nose glued to the ground and a good head of steam, and I wondered if he'd run right into my tree.

I know now I should have waited, but patience was not one of my strong points. When my first shot whistled by him, that buck skidded to a halt, lifted his head and looked around wondering what happened. The second ounce of lead slamming into a tree behind him spurred the buck on a mad dash right past my twisted old oak. Four more times I shucked the pump as the buck blew by.

He was gone, and I sat in the tree shaking like a whipped pup.

Ten minutes later, I climbed down from the tree for a look around. I would have bet my shotgun I had missed, but Pa was a stickler about not wasting game, and he had taught me to always look for sign of a hit.

The half-dozen, scattered, green hulls on the ground, smoking reminders of the debacle, made me sink even lower as I took up the track of the buck. Following the path of his hasty flight was easy across the frosty leaves. When I came upon the crimson splash on both sides of his track, though, I let out a whoop like a Bluetick pup on a hot coon scent. In my excitement, I nearly tripped over the buck sprawled in the leaves only 50 yards away.

Since Then...

Since that day a quarter century past, I've used gallons of deer scent. I've dripped, dragged, sprayed and stomped deer urine from South Texas to the northern extreme of whitetail range in Canada and a dozen or so states in between. Deer scents have worked their magic for me often enough over the years that you won't find me in the woods without them.

Yet, I'll be the first to preach that deer scents won't hide sloppy hunting tactics. What scents can do for you is help you bring in that buck you otherwise would never see. Used correctly, scents can help mask your own odor and give you those precious extra seconds we so desperately need to get off a good shot.

When I'm bowhunting, I use scents to help position the deer right where I want it for the shot. Scents can make a deer decoy smell like the real thing and sometimes work wonders in combination with rattling and calling. But like rattling, calling, decoys and other hunting aids, scents don't work all the time.

Expect miracles and you'll quickly become disappointed. Accept scents as another method that can improve your odds and you'll probably end up like me—checking your pockets to make sure you have a bottle of scent before heading into the woods.

What Kind Of Scent To Use

What should that bottle have in it? Depends on how you're trying to fool the deer's nose.

Back when I began using scents, there were two choices—deer urine and fox urine. I bought fox urine in pint bottles from the fur buyer for years before I ever saw small bottles of fox urine intended for deer hunters. Fox urine was my cover scent and deer urine was the lure. Today's choices are more complex.

We writers have contributed to that confusion by grouping scents into only two categories, cover scents and attractants. Scent science becomes clearer if we recognize four categories: cover scents, food attractants, gland-based lures and deer urine scents.

Under Cover

A cover scent is anything you put on your clothing or near your stand to mask your human odor. Fox urine, coon urine and some tree or earth scents are the most common.

Most of us overdo it with cover scents. A cover scent cannot eliminate your human odor. Instead, it is intended to hide that odor well enough to confuse the olfactory signals a downwind deer receives. Sometimes it works well enough to allow time for a clean, killing shot.

If you take the "more is better" approach and slather on the cover scent, you defeat the purpose. Deer are accustomed to smelling fox urine, for example, in small doses. A couple of drops is all you want.

Choose a cover scent common to the area you hunt. You are trying to calm the deer by presenting an odor they smell every day of their lives and do not associate with danger. That's why my all-time favorite cover scent is a fresh cow pie. What better cover scent in areas where deer live near cattle? At least one company now markets a cattle cover scent, and I'm betting others will follow suit.

Apple Pie, Not Cow Pie

It's a mistake to lump a bunch of other scents under the category of cover scents, when they're really food attractant scents. A partial list would include apple, acorn, sweet corn, honeysuckle and persimmon. The whole idea behind a cover scent is that it be something the deer is used to smelling and is not attracted to. Smells that deer associate with food defeat the purpose.

Since scents like apple and persimmon are intended to attract deer, don't put them on yourself nor very close to your stand. Instead, use food attractant scents in locations around your stand that will help position the deer for a good shot opportunity.

Before using food attractant scents, be sure to check out the laws on baiting in the state you are hunting. In some locations putting out anything the deer might be inclined to eat qualifies as bait.

Glands Hold Scent Secrets

Gland-based lures are the latest craze among deer scent companies. Produced from the tarsal, interdigital, forehead, preorbital or metatarsal gland, each is designed with a specific purpose in mind. Scents that incorporate tarsal gland, for instance, are an excellent choice for doctoring scrapes. The combination of buck urine and tarsal gland mimics the communication behavior of a buck when he squats and urinates over a scrape. Early in the pre-rut, bucks often

Doe-in-heat scent has been the demise of many white-tailed bucks. Still, the best scent can't disguise sloppy hunting techniques.

urinate in scrapes with their legs splayed. However, as the rut gets closer they almost always stand in the scrape with tarsal glands together and urinate through them into the scrape.

My favorite scent system starts with peeling the tarsal glands from a freshly killed buck during the rut. If any of my buddies takes a mature, rutting buck before I do, I always go over and have a look, tell him what a dandy the deer is, and make off with the tarsal glands.

I leave one tarsal as is and put the other in a Zip-Loc bag with half an ounce of doe-in-estrus urine. After slicing a hole in each tarsal, I tie them with a string and drag them or sometimes tie one to each boot. I lay down a scent trail while hiking into my stand and will sometimes loop past the stand and back again. This improves the odds of a buck crossing the trail and turning in my direction. Assuming my stand is facing directly upwind, I hang one tarsal from a bush or limb 20 yards to my right and the other the same distance to my left. Any buck catching whiff is likely to investigate—especially if I've done an adequate job of eliminating my own human scent.

Many times I've witnessed bucks sniff and lick the tarsal glands. One buck even tore a tarsal from the bush where I had hung it. He proceeded to rake the tarsal on the ground with his antlers.

The interdigital gland is small and located between the split hooves of a deer. The gland secretes a waxy substance, and it is believed that scent left from the interdigital gland helps deer follow each other. Thus, scents using the interdigital gland are also great for leaving scent trails you want the deer to follow.

Rubs and the overhanging branch at a scrape are important visual signposts for deer, but scent at these important locations appears to be at least equally important in whitetail communication. The forehead gland and pre-orbital gland come into play on rubs and on overhanging branches at scrapes. When a buck rubs a tree with his antlers, the exposed cambium layer of the tree is obvious to the eye. But the scent left by the buck's forehead gland, preorbital gland and even his saliva are the animal's signature—the way he identifies himself to other deer.

It's been my experience that bucks are attracted to mock rubs whether or not the rub has been doctored with scent. However, a buck could be enticed to stay in the vicinity longer if a scent is used on the rub.

Basically, the same holds true when using forehead gland and preorbital gland scent on the overhanging branch of mock scrapes or existing scrapes. Many times when a buck comes to a scrape, he focuses most of his attention on the branch rather than the scrape itself.

Early in November last year, I was hunting in western Illinois and made a mock scrape 12 steps in front of my tree stand. I doctored the scrape and overhanging branch with scent. The first day I sat in the stand, six different bucks checked it. All were immature bucks—yearlings and 2½-year-olds. Interestingly, however, none of the six urinated in the scrape or even pawed at it. All six, though, smelled and licked the overhanging branch. Four of them rubbed their faces and antlers on the branch.

The small metatarsal gland is covered by white hairs and located low on the outside of each hind leg. Scent from the metatarsal gland is released only when a deer becomes alarmed. At least one scent manufacturer has taken the metatarsal gland, combined it with human fatty acids and created a scent intended to repel deer. By placing the scent along other trails it is thought that hunters can funnel deer closer to stand locations. Still, some research indicates the metatarsal gland neither repels nor attracts other whitetails (Volkman 1981).

Deer Urine Scents

This is the largest category of deer scents and the one with which most hunters have had some experience. Buck urine, doe urine, doe-in-estrus urine (often call doe-in-heat scent) and fawn urine are usually sold in liquid form, but you can also find them as a gel, powder, patch, solid wafer or even send them up as smoke or vapor.

There is a common assumption that doe-in-estrus urine should be used only during the rut, while the other urine scents are better suited for use during pre-rut and post-rut. The contention is that using the doe-in-estrus urine at any time other than during the rut will alert rather than attract deer. This assumes that deer know that the time is not right for them to be smelling the scent of a doe-in-estrus and so they become suspicious. I don't buy it.

I've been using doe-in-estrus lures for two decades. During that time, I've used them from September to January while hunting whitetails across North America. Never have I seen any evidence of doe-in-estrus lure spooking a buck regardless of the season. True, I have found these lures to be most effective during the scraping period and actual breeding season, but I've also enjoyed good results long before and long after the rut.

Remember, a white-tailed buck is capable of breeding from the time he sheds the velvet from his antlers right up until he drops his headgear. During that period any buck catching a whiff of doe-in-estrus scent is a candidate for your freezer. I've watched them sniff the scent and ignore it. I've observed as bucks have inhaled the scent, showed mild interest and then went on about their business. And, on many occasions, I've seen them become slaves to the tantalizing aroma. I've never seen it spook them.

The only problem I've ever had while using doe-in-estrus lure has been from does. Often I've had does smell my trail of doe-in-estrus scent and instantly go on full alert. Stomping their front hooves and snorting are other doe behaviors I've witnessed while using doe-in-estrus scent. If a buck is nearby, this can spell disaster. Still, in my experience, the positives have seemed to outweigh the negatives.

The only time I switch from a doe-in-estrus urine to urine collected from a non-estrus doe is when I'm not hunting strictly for a buck. If I have an antlerless-only permit, regular doe or fawn urine is a better choice.

I don't really see the need for buck urine. You might be able to pique a buck's territorial instincts by laying down a trail of buck urine, but a buck is more inclined to follow a trail of doe-in-estrus than buck urine. Ditto for using buck urine in scrapes. My results with this technique have been disappointing. You can't blame a buck for looking for a receptive doe instead of a fight with another buck.

Scents can help you to see more deer, attract larger bucks, avoid detection by downwind deer, more accurately predict the direction of a deer's approach and position a buck for the shot. Scents make sense.

3

Calling All Deer

by John Phillips

Grunting, snorting and bleating are among the hottest tactics in deer hunting. The techniques that waterfowl, turkey and elk hunters have used for years are now being applied by deer hunters across North America with great success.

There's nothing mystical about deer calling; it's simply using the sounds deer normally make in the woods to entice them near your stand. The technique, even when mastered, is not a cure-all to hunting woes, but instead is simply another strategy the serious, well-prepared hunter can pull from his bag of tricks.

The Sounds Deer Make

What is a hunter saying to a deer when he blows a call? What calls are the most effective? What is communicated by the different sounds that the hunter attempts to imitate?

Almost every hunter and call manufacturer has speculated about these questions, but a group of scientists in Athens, Georgia, is searching for answers. Dr. Larry Marchinton, head of the University of Georgia's Deer Research Project, shared his research on deer vocalization.

"First of all we have to define deer vocalization as sounds that deer make to communicate with one another," Marchinton explained. "We're just in the infant stages of learning how deer communicate. So at this point, we're trying to learn what questions to ask about deer communication rather than coming up with hard-formed conclusions. Although deer may very well have a language, we don't know this for sure.

"Deer vocalization is a relatively new area of investigation. The first papers containing scientific data on the topic were published in 1981—one by a gentleman named Richardson at the University of Michigan, and the other by Tom Atkinson for his Ph.D. dissertation at the University of Georgia.

"From these papers and the resulting research, biologists now know that deer communicate a lot of information through the sounds they make. They can communicate alarm, aggression, the desire to make contact, as well as calls between the mothers and fathers and fawns, and many more that we don't know about at this time."

Marchinton went on to identify the different calls that deer make and tell us what they mean.

Distress Calls

"Two calls indicate distress—the snort and the bawl," Marchinton reported. "Most hunters have heard the snort, which is an alarm call that deer use. I personally believe that the snort communicates danger in the area. Some research tends to indicate that when a deer snorts, he's trying to solicit some type of response from the animal or person at which he is snorting. When a deer snorts, it often senses danger, which may mean that it's using this type of communication to try and make a predator show itself.

"But there are no easy definitions of what deer sounds mean. I have a graduate student named Grant Woods who works in my department. Woods has been utilizing the snort to call deer in. If the snort was strictly an alarm call, then it wouldn't be able to lure deer. However, Woods has been able to do just that. We're still learning a great deal.

"The bawl, which is a cry of pain, can be made on a modified predator call. The bawl is an effective call for the hunter to call up does. Occasionally I've seen a buck come to the bawl, but this call apparently stimulates the maternal response of the deer. Although the bawl seems to be most productive right after fawning season, deer will come to this call even in the fall."

Antagonistic Or Aggressive Sounds

"There are basically three of these calls given by the mature buck,"

Marchinton reported. "There's the grunt, the grunt/snort and the grunt/snort/wheeze, the most aggressive call that a deer vocalizes, is made with a grunt followed by one to four snorts, and then a wheeze. When a deer gives this call, he's telling another deer or the animals that are threatening him that he's serious and something is going to happen."

Mating Calls

"The grunt call that hunters use most often does not fall into the category of aggressive calls, but comes under the heading of tending or mating calls," Marchinton said. "The tending grunt is more drawn out and the sound of the grunt actually lasts longer than the aggressive grunt. The aggressive grunt is shorter and sharper than the tending grunt. The tending grunt is the call that the deer voices when he's tending a doe. But even if hunters get these two calls confused, the grunt may still have the same effect of drawing in a buck, because a buck may come to the call either to fight or to mate.

"The grunt call, whether a tending grunt or an aggressive grunt, may also run off a subordinate buck. The aggressive grunt almost always will scare off a subordinate buck, but the tending grunt may draw in a subordinate buck that hopes he may be able to breed the doe that's with the other buck.

"The phlegm and sniff is a kind of squeaky noise that the deer makes when he curls his lip up. This call usually is given by a buck when he first smells estrus urine. And often bucks will give this call whether the urine is estrus or not."

The Contact Call

"The contact call is given primarily by does and fawns of both sexes. This, too, is a type of grunt. But this contact call is longer than the threatening grunt and not quite as low as the other grunts. Rather, the contact call is higher pitched because it's made by the does and the fawns. The contact call seems to tell other deer, 'I'm over here. Come find me.' Quite often I've heard this call given by fawns that are separated from does.

"Scientists have learned that the grunt call in its various levels of intensity and different tones is used by deer to communicate many things at different times, which is perhaps one of the reasons that commercial grunt calls often tend to be effective for hunters. Even if you give the wrong grunt call, you still may lure in the deer.

"For instance, if you intend to give a tending grunt, but don't know the difference between a tending and an aggressive grunt, and the sound you give communicates aggression, you still may call in a deer. Instead of calling in a buck that may want to mate, you may call in a buck that prefers to fight, which is what makes deer calling so different from other types of animal calling. If you give the wrong call when you're duck or turkey calling, more than likely you'll spook the game—but not when calling deer."

Fawn Calls

"The mew is a high-pitched call that's not as loud as the bleat," Marchinton explained. "The mew seems to be a call that the fawn uses to solicit the attention of the doe. Also a juvenile utilizes the mew to keep from getting lost or just to be recognized.

"The bleat is louder than a mew, longer than the mew, and much more intense. The fawns often will use the bleat when they want to feed. The bleat is quite similar to a contact call and is often used by the hunter to say to the deer, 'Hello, I'm over here. Come find me.'

"The nursing whine is a sound fawns vocalize when they're nursing or when they want to nurse."

Marchinton On Techniques for Calling

"I believe that hunters are now beginning to understand and effectively use deer calls," Marchinton observed. "Whether we'll ever reach the level of communication that a duck hunter has when he calls in a flight of ducks is still speculative. Remember, deer have bigger brains than ducks and are not fooled quite as easily."

Besides being a deer researcher, Marchinton is also an avid deer hunter. When asked if he used deer calls he answered, "Occasionally. I play with all the calls to see what kind of results I'll get. But the call I utilize most is the tending grunt. I use my mouth to call deer most of the time rather than the commercial calls.

"I also use deer calls in conjunction with rattling. A call that I feel can be very effective is what I call the straining grunt. Hunters acquainted with the technique of hunting deer known as rattling understand that clashing the antlers simulates two bucks fighting. I know they give off a grunting sound similar to that made by two opposing linemen when they try to push and shove each other out of the way to make a hole for the running back. So I call this grunt the straining grunt, which is a deep guttural sound that's somewhere between a roar and a grunt.

"Although on several occasions I've called deer in using this call, I'm sure at other times I've turned deer off with it. The key to using this grunt successfully is to put a strained sound in the call. A hunter must realize that this call may scare off any deer except the most dominant buck in the area.

"The key to successful deer calling is to use the correct call at the right time of the year. For instance, the most effective time to use the tending grunt is during breeding season. In the early part of hunting season, if you want to call in a doe, then common sense tells you to use some fawn in distress contact calls. If you're hunting in an area where the buck-to-doe ratio is so out of balance that there aren't many bucks, and you want to harvest a doe, then rattle. In regions with few bucks but numerous does, the does will respond to anything that sounds like a buck, especially in the latter part of the season. However, calling in bucks is extremely difficult when there are more does than bucks.

"Where there is a more balanced buck/doe ratio and some older bucks are in the herd, then rattling becomes a very effective way to call one in. Or you can use the tending grunt in these places, especially after most the does have been bred, to call in a buck. Many areas of the nation have deer herds so out of balance that there are far more does than bucks. So often the bucks in these regions don't seem to respond to any forms of calling nearly as well."

Rattling

To give an overview of deer calling, we must not only mention deer vocalization but also take a passing look at rattling antlers. Marchinton feels that antler rattling falls into two categories: sparring matches and buck fights.

According to Marchinton, "Sparring matches, which are not true fights, usually take place early in the season, right after the velvet is shed from the buck's antlers. During this testing time, each buck learns its position in the herd, and deer form their pecking order. As the season progresses and the does go into the rut, there often will be full-blown fights. The fights occur when two dominant bucks or two bucks that think they're dominant come into conflict because of a doe. This is when the all-out battle occurs.

"Once you understand the difference in the two types of deer fights, you have to adapt the severity of your rattling techniques to the time of the year you're hunting. If you're hunting early in deer season when the bucks are forming their pecking order, then tickling the antlers—just lightly hitting the tips together nearly as hard as you will later in the season—is best. If you're rattling during the rut, you need to clash the antlers together with a lot of force and grunt to simulate a full-blown buck fight.

The sound of two bucks fighting can attract both bucks and does. Bucks also grunt during these fights.

"But once again, rattling antlers is not a sure-fire way to bring in a dominant buck. I've seen dominant bucks that were tending does actually veer away from fights. Researchers believe that they move away from a fight to keep from losing the doe that they're tending."

Although information about deer vocalization and deer calling will make you more knowledgeable about the deer you hunt, all hunters should remember that deer calling is not a magic cure-all. Calling deer doesn't replace knowledge of the animal or woodsmanship. The ability to call deer is just another aid that on certain days, under specific conditions, may bring a buck to the hunter.

The Instruments Of Deer Calling

Since the scientific community has begun to identify different types of deer vocalization, many call manufacturers have started to make products that imitate those vocalizations. High-tech audio equipment is used to determine the frequency and the pitch of a real deer's sounds. Then call manufacturers attempt to build calls that match the frequency and pitch of the deer's vocalization.

Since not all deer sound just alike, neither do all calls make the same sound. How then can sportsmen decide which calls are best? Depending on which call manufacturer you talk to, they all can make a solid case for why a hunter needs a grunt call, a wheeze call and/or a bleat call. But which call is best for you, your type of hunting, the area where you hunt, and why?

Among scientists, expert hunters, and call manufacturers, it seems universally accepted that the tending grunt has the greatest potential to lure bucks within range.

Perhaps the main reason the grunt call is so effective is because this call can be used to communicate several messages to a buck deer that will cause him to come to the hunter. The grunt call communicates aggression, socialization and the buck's need for sex. When a buck deer gives a tending grunt, he's letting all the other bucks in the woods know that there's a doe in estrus in the region and he's following her. Therefore, if a hunter blows on a grunt call, even if he doesn't know what the various types of grunts mean, he may still be able to attract a buck.

There are numerous kinds of grunt calls. The first grunt call, like the first caller used for turkeys, was simply a hunter imitating a deer's call with his own mouth. Then one day someone, somewhere found that turning around a duck call and sucking on it would produce a grunt like a deer's. And finally, someone discovered that putting a flexible tube on the end of that duck call would even more closely reproduce the sound of a grunting deer.

The words, "depending on who you talk to," must be included when describing the origin of the grunt call because most every call manufacturer seems to make some claim on the invention.

Although grunt calls come in different sizes, shapes and materials with various lengths of hose on them or no hose at all, and although call manufacturers will attempt to prove that their grunt call works the best, biologists and avid deer hunters will tell you that most grunt calls work, no matter whose label is on them.

The old bass fisherman's adage, "A spinner bait is a spinner bait is a spinner bait" also may be true of grunt calls for deer. Actually, the hunter who takes any grunt call, masters it, and has confidence in it, should be able to call deer with that call.

Apparently more research has been done on the grunt call of the deer than on the other calls. Researchers and hunters believe if they had only one call to use to call deer, it would be the grunt call. The bleat call and the wheeze call are productive calls, but don't seem to be as effective in every location and throughout the season as is the grunt call.

Copying Nature's Wonders

Another calling method that has proven to be deadly in luring bucks is antler rattling and the whole array of sounds that the hunter can make when he's clashing antlers together. Rattling antlers also come in many forms and are produced by numerous manufacturers. Some rattling antlers aren't manufactured, but rather are antlers that have been picked up by sportsmen or purchased by suppliers from hunters or game farms. (Use caution as not all states permit the buying and selling of deer antlers.)

A second type are produced from synthetics, usually molded plastic, to resemble deer antlers. Bob Zaiglin, a wildlife biologist and designer of both the Lynch and the Eastman rattling antlers, explains that "There are some drawbacks with using natural antlers to rattle for deer. The brow tines are knuckle busters when the hunter clashes antlers together. And when the hunter uses a left antler and a right antler, he may also bash his hands together when he brings the horns together.

"Therefore, in developing the rattling antlers that I use, I eliminated the brow tines and made both antlers right-handed antlers. Then the antlers can be clashed together back to back, and the hunter is not nearly as likely to beat-up and bloody-up his hands.

"Although most of my rattling has been done with real antlers in years past, I can tell absolutely no difference in the effectiveness of the synthetic antlers. I am also convinced that they're much safer to use. Not only do I not get as beat-up with the synthetic antlers as I did with the real things, my synthetic antlers are green—not the color of real antlers."

Another type of rattling antlers that many manufacturers are producing is the rattling bags, which contain pieces of plastic that when rubbed together shaken or crashed in the sides of trees while still in the bag sound much like the real thing. Besides being easier to carry, the rattling bags are more camouflaged than the rattling antlers. And once again, depending on who you talk to, manufacturers of each believe that their particular product is the best. And Lohman produces several rattling boxes that allow one-handed operation of the call.

However, there's more involved in rattling than the sounds of antlers clashing. Many of the hunters who've been highly successful in using rattling to call in deer also beat the nearby ground with the antlers, scrape the antlers up and down the sides of trees and use the antlers to hook bushes.

If rattling antlers, rattling bags, rattling boxes and grunt calls appear to be the best types of calls to lure in whitetails, then combining these calls may in fact be the very best way to bring a deer to your crosshairs.

It seems the grunt call is most effective when a deer is within 100 yards of the hunter. Rattling appears to be a long-range call that the hunter can utilize to pull deer from more that 100 yards away. But remember when trying to select calls to aid you in your hunting that the calls are just that—aids.

Advanced Deer-Calling Strategies

Sporting goods dealers will be the first to point out to you that there are more magical devices available to the deer hunter than ever before. Magical calls, wonder-working scents, mystical lures, spell-binding horns, floating tree stands and invisible camo patterns will bewitch you as you stroll down the aisle of your favorite sporting goods emporium. Unfortunately you may find the array bewildering as well.

All the advertisers of these products would have you believe that if you buy their brand of magic, you can conjure a domestic buck into range of your bow or rifle. Avoid any salesman who comes on like the patent medicine barker who claims that one product does it all. There is not single hunting tool or gimmick that will replace good solid hunting technique.

Remember, the deer call is just one more tool the hunter can use to help him take his buck. It is not the ultimate tool or the only tool! A good hunter and woodsman without a deer call will always harvest more deer than a rookie with one. However, a good hunter with a deer call should be able to bag his buck more consistently than a skilled hunter without one.

Let's walk through a hunt plan considering the proven factors for successful deer hunting and put the deer call in its proper perspective within the planned hunt.

The Lay Of The Land

A hunter who tries to take a deer without a thorough knowledge of the land is like a blind man at a track meet. Although he may reach the goal, he will be a long time arriving there. On the other hand, he may never get there.

Aerial photos and topo maps of the land you plan to hunt are critical tools to the hunter because they not only give a visual representation of the area, but also show direction, which is important to a hunt plan.

For instance, if you know a northwesterly wind is blowing, but you're not sure in which direction you must walk to reach a stand site, you could be moving to your stand with the wind at your back and have your human odor carried into your hunting area before your reach your stand. The hunter who is familiar with the land and listens to weather radio each morning can determine which areas to hunt and which sites the wind will not permit him to hunt.

Maps also allow you to find spots that are hard to reach, as well as overlooked places in the woods where others may not have hunted.

From ground observation, the woods-wise outdoorsman should be able to determine where deer are feeding, bedding and moving. You'll see where bucks are scraping, whether there is a big buck in the area and where good stand sites are located. Without this information, the best deer call in the world rarely, if ever, will produce a buck.

Don't Spook The Deer You're Trying To Take

Once you've located an area to hunt, you have to prevent spooking the deer you're attempting to call. If the wind is wrong to hunt a certain area, don't hunt that spot until the wind is right.

By now enough has been written about the effect of the wind on the deer hunting that there is little need to belabor the point. However, not enough has been written about how the hunter approaches his stand and sets up his tree stand. The stalk to the stand should be as slow and deliberate as a stalk to the deer. The hunter cannot assume that the deer is not watching him.

Although the buck's number one danger detector is his nose, he also has the ability to see and hear well. Therefore, a slow, quiet, deliberate stalk to the stand is essential to successful deer hunting. Many a trophy buck has been harvested by a hunter while moving quietly to his deer stand.

One mistake hunters make in deer calling is to blow their deer calls on the way to their stands. The logic goes, "If calls are supposed to bring in deer, then why not blow them every 10 or 15 minutes?" But, this is about as appropriate as saying, "Since my gun is on my shoulder, and it's supposed to kill deer, why not shoot it every 10 to 15 minutes? Maybe I'll hit something!"

There is a time and a place for everything. The time to utilize a deer call is when and where you expect to see a deer, and you are prepared to take him, just like the time to use a rifle is only when you have a whitetail in your sights.

If the hunter uses cover scents, the stalk to the stand is the best place to use the scents. But don't disregard the wind.

Be sure you know the difference in cover scents and deer lures. Cover scents supposedly mask human odor, while deer attractants draw deer to the hunter. So you don't want to draw deer to you until you reach your stand. Therefore, only use cover scents on the way to the stand and deer lures once you reach the stand.

Use Deer Lures To Your Advantage

No deer lure always attracts deer, and no deer call always calls deer. However, because of a deer's natural curiosity, often a deer will come in when it smells a deer lure.

Always place the lure about waist-high on limbs or bushes so the aroma will be at about the same height as a deer's nose. In the mornings, you may want to put the lure closer to the ground because of the rising air currents called "thermals" that actually will lift the scent into the air. Since thermals in the late afternoon cause a downward movement of air, the scents often should be placed a little higher at that time.

Deer lures often can be the factor that brings the buck even closer to the stand than the deer call does, because once a deer hears a deer call and comes in, he expects to see and smell another deer. Deer lures may be most effective for the bowhunter or the blackpowder shooter who must have a close shot.

The Right Call At The Right Time

All deer calls have a specific effective range and knowing that range is an important factor in the efficiency of calling. For instance, the grunt, bleat, and wheeze calls are only effective about 50 to 100 yards, but on a still day they may be heard for greater distances. Therefore, if the hunter has stalked quietly and successfully to his stand and has given the woods a few minutes to settle, he should use these calls first to call in deer that are close by.

After calling, waiting 15 minutes, calling again, and not seeing a deer, he may assume there are not deer within hearing range. The hunter may then want to use rattling antlers to attempt to call a deer that may be a greater distance from his stand. If the hunter rattles up a buck, but the deer won't come close enough for a shot or is standing in thick cover, he may use a grunt call to bring the buck even closer.

If a buck is spotted running at 150 or so yards from the stand, the hunter may be able to clash antlers to stop the buck for a shot. But if the deer is moving through spotty cover at 50 to 60 yards from the hunter's stand, blowing the grunt call may be a better tool for stopping the buck.

Although we've primarily discussed utilizing deer calls to lure in bucks, deer calls will also call does, because all deer are curious. So an unusual sound will cause a doe as well as a buck to come in and investigate what made the sound. Deer are social critters, too, and often desire the company of their own kind.

A favorite story about calling up does is told by a friend, Sam Spencer: "I was rattling when all of a sudden two does appeared. I could tell by their actions that they definitely had come in to the sound of the rattling antlers. As I studied the does, I began to wonder why they had come to what sounded like a buck fight. All I could determine was what they were two ladies on the prowl who had heard two males who might want company!"

Know Why Calls Don't Work

For every one time a deer call is responsible for producing a buck, there are two to five times that it will not. As with any hunting technique, the list of reasons calling won't work is long. And none of these reasons are anything the hunter has complete control over:

1. There are no deer in the area to hear the call.

2. The deer don't want to be social.

3. The dominant buck already has an estrus doe with him and doesn't want to risk losing her in a fight.

4. The buck has fought just recently and is not ready for another war.

5. The buck is a subordinate buck and does not want to challenge the dominant buck.

6. The hunter is not saying what the buck wants to hear.

The hunter who consistently uses a deer call will take more deer if he is also a knowledgeable hunter.

But remember, the deer call is not a magical flute. It is not a magic wand that will make a deer appear if there's not a deer within hearing range. It is not a substitute for good hunting technique.

4

Hunting The Nocturnal Buck

by Larry Weishuhn

*T*he moon was a thin, silver sliver in the dark November sky. The brisk northerly wind made the night seem much colder. Legal shooting hours had been over for nearly seven hours. I glanced over at my partner, Ron Porter, then a game warden with the New Mexico Department of Game & Fish. "Is it time?" he asked. I nodded an affirmative. With that we left camp and headed off into the darkness.

The purpose was to conduct a nighttime spotlight game survey and to observe white-tailed bucks on one of the ranches I had under an intensive quality deer management program. The ranch also served as a white-tailed deer research area.

Earlier in the day, a local Texas game warden had been informed of our nighttime activity and invited to accompany us. Occasionally he did, but tonight he was busy elsewhere.

We began seeing deer almost immediately upon setting out, and they were different deer from those we had seen during the daytime. Most notably we saw several bucks, and not just run of the mill bucks, but some of the biggest bucks on the ranch. This included four monstrous bucks that I had very rarely seen during daylight hours. For the most part I had seen them only during these nighttime surveys and even then only during the hours of 1:30 a.m. to 3:30 a.m. In the past I had, on occasion, found one or more of their shed antlers. Yet, the deer had never been seen during the daylight hours by anyone other than me.

As I mentioned, the ranch, approximately 1,000 acres in size, was intensively managed to produce big whitetails. It was surrounded by an 8-foot mesh wire fence, not so much to keep the deer in, but to keep deer from neighboring properties out. Otherwise the management benefits to the deer on the property would have been greatly diminished. The deer inside the high fence had everything they needed and wanted to eat, in terms of native browse, supplemental feed available in troughs 24 hours a day throughout the year, and planted food plots that had been fertilized. They wanted for nothing!

Throughout the hunting season there were hunters in the field nearly every day. Each year we harvested a considerable number of does, and a quota of bucks based on deer densities, fawn survival rates, buck-to-doe ratios and long-term management goals. The latter included producing the very finest and largest bucks.

The hunters were required to keep detailed records of does, fawns and bucks they observed while in the field. In the case of the latter, number of points, spread, mass and, if possible, a photo or video record was also included. None of the hunters ever reported seeing any of the four bucks we saw that night. That did not surprise me. In my opinion, these particular deer could truly be classified as nocturnal bucks. And those four were not the only bucks on the ranch that adopted nocturnal behavior as they matured.

Another of our nocturnal bucks was one that had been bottle-raised by the ranch foreman and his wife, and for the first year of its life was a pet. When the buck turned 4 years old, the only time he was seen was after dark. He had large tags in his ears so he was plainly marked and should have been easy to identify. All of this makes me wonder how many totally nocturnal bucks there are in any deer population.

Deer tend to move for one or both of two reasons, hunger or sex. Several of the totally nocturnal bucks I kept tabs on fed only at night, and they also tended to chase does only after dark. Is there a chink in the armor of these bucks, or are they the bucks that are simply unkillable?

In the case of the bucks inside the 1,000-acre enclosure, they were extremely familiar with their habitat. When hunters were on the ranch the bucks simply did not move during daylight hours, or when they did it was when the hunters were back at camp. Had I not shown the owner and his family the deer after dark, they likely would not have believed such huge bucks existed on the property.

I mentioned deer "move" for one of two reasons. In the case of this particular ranch, the deer had more than plenty to eat. The food was available 24 hours per day, and they did not have to hustle to fill their rumens. They could eat a belly full in a matter of a few minutes, any time of the day or night. Unless the rut was going on, the sex drive of the nocturnal bucks did not come into play. What I noticed, however, was that the nocturnal bucks on that ranch, and several other operations I have dealt with, tend to be at least 5 years old or older. They generally had extremely good antler development.

They also did not appear to be particularly sexually active. If a willing doe happened to enter the home area of one of these bucks, he might pursue her as long as she stayed in the thick brush. But, if she left the safety of the cover in his core area, he would not follow. Regardless of the urges or circumstances, with those particular bucks, the urge to survive was stronger than anything else— including the urge to procreate.

I suspect there are nocturnal bucks, such as those mentioned, throughout the whitetail's range. According to biologists, wardens, guides and outfitters and hunters I have talked to throughout the country, they tend to agree. In most every instance, the nocturnal bucks they describe tend to have huge antlers, generally among the best to be found in the respective areas.

Are such bucks impossible to take? I think in some instances they might be. When most finally do die, it is from natural causes or they meet their end by a vehicle on a highway in the wee hours of the morning. Or they are taken by a novice hunter who does not know that the unkillable nocturnal bucks cannot be taken.

Perhaps therein lies the chink in the armor of the nocturnal super buck. Many of the biggest bucks are taken by rather inexperienced hunters, or by those who had no prior knowledge of a buck of huge proportions in the area. The inexperienced hunter does not know these bucks are "supposed" to live in only the worst of thickets or in areas farthest from "civilization." Thus, they hunt near major roadways, or very close to camp. They do not know you are supposed to hunt big bucks in only the thickest of cover, and avoid the relatively open fields. They do not know you are not supposed to try to rattle up a buck, well before the beginning of the rut. Neither do they know you are only supposed to hunt early in the morning and late in the afternoon.

After many years of dealing with big bucks, I have learned deer tend to pattern hunters! Within the outdoor journals written about hunting whitetails it has become popular to pontificate about patterning whitetails. What most of these writers do not realize is that while they are patterning the deer, the deer, especially mature bucks, are patterning them! I have seen this happen many different times, in a great variety of deer habitat.

Nocturnal bucks occasionally slip up. Usually these deer are 5 years old or older.

Matching wits with a monster whitetail is great fun, and certainly a challenge. But, "do not out-think yourself," as a friend of mine who has taken numerous trophy bucks likes to say. According to him, there is a problem with falling into a rut when you hunt the nocturnal buck.

You hunt the same general area day after day and use the same techniques as others. He advises to dare to be different. One of the best bucks he has taken came from what appeared to be an open field, declared as deerless by his fellow hunters. But right in the middle of the huge grassy field was a depression, and unless you walked through the field you would never know it was there. My friend found it while on a mourning dove hunt. What he also found there were several deer beds and one set of huge deer tracks. About three months later, he left camp four hours before daylight and found a comfortable place to wait in the middle of the depression, in the middle of the field. Just before first light he heard a deer approach the area and bed down. When legal shooting light finally arrived, he shot a monstrous, typical 12-point at 40 feet.

Back at camp the landowner came by to look at the deer. According to him, he had seen the buck numerous times, but always at night when it crossed the road in front of his pickup, or feeding in a field, while the rancher checked his cattle.

When I have seen nocturnal bucks during daylight hours, it has consistently been close to noon. Our hunters were in camp eating or resting, because they believed deer only moved early and late. Wrong! I have seen more big bucks during the middle of the day than any other time. Deer that tend to move during the middle of the night also tend to move during the middle of the day. Knowing that one bit of deer behavior helped me take my biggest typical to date.

That buck was taken at 11:35 a.m., after a night when the moon was full.

If you want to take a nocturnal buck, be willing to hunt all day, and hunt in areas that are avoided by others because they are, "too open," "too close to camp," or "too close to a road." Find such unhunted pockets and you just might find the hiding place of the nocturnal buck.

5

You Can Trail Trophy Whitetail

by Jeff Murray

*F*or trophy deer hunters such as Noble Carlson, trailing deer is a science. It was Carlson who told me I was spreading myths when I said there is no single, reliable method to tell a buck's track from a large doe's.

"All you've got are theories," he said. "I've got the facts. I spend most almost as much time in the woods as the deer during the fall, except I don't sleep out there."

The fact that he's harvested more than 100 bucks is more than incidental trivia, but simply shooting a lot of deer doesn't give him instant credibility. It's how Carlson takes the majority of his white-tail trophies that really focused my attention and should attract yours. Carlson tracked them down!

To get the inside story on trailing trophy whitetails, I hunted with Carlson one-on-one on his northern Minnesota home turf. Here's what I discovered.

On The Trail With Noble Carlson

Carlson was stopped dead in his tracks. "Shh!" he whispered. His blue Scandinavian eyes lowered beneath bristly, bleached-orange eyebrows.

Moments earlier, we had been half-trotting square down a deer trail. Noble himself had loudly snapped three twigs. I heard them easily, and I was counting. Now he was yapping at me to be totally silent.

Tracking deer, Noble Carlson style, was weird.

"That buzzard," he said. "I'm starting to get mad." We stood next to the fresh deer bed. "We must have spooked him."

Under normal circumstances, Noble would leave the buck alone. From nearly 30 years of tracking whitetails, he has learned that it is usually futile to stay on top of a spooked buck; they'll outrun you most every time. But this was different. He knelt down, sized up the bed and asked me if I wanted the buck.

As a devout stand hunter, I've tolerated too many days when deer weren't moving. If I could track bucks on those days, I could be a lot more effective and successful.

"Look," he said. "You aren't even sure whether this is a buck or doe, are you? But I know. Get a sniff of this."

He tossed me a chunk of stained yellow snow. It was rancid, musky, all male. I was convinced.

"Look at the width of the track," he said. "See how deep it penetrates the snow? And the tips are rounded off pretty good. No young buck has round tips like these. If you want to go for it, I can guarantee a 50-50 shot, but you gotta do exactly what I say."

Telling Buck Tracks From Doe Tracks

The next time you see a deer track, study it careful. There are simple methods to determine whether the track was made by a buck or doe.

"Every buck track shares certain characteristics that clearly distinguish it from a doe's," says Carlson. "What first strikes you about the track of a big buck is how the hoof-print arcs out from the tip like an upside-down Valentine's heart. A doe's print is much different. Instead of a blunt tip and a broad wide arc, does' hooves don't curve much before they angle down to the bottom of the pad. The size of the track…has little to do with it. Even a little buck's tracks arc out from the tip."

When you find a sharp deer track, whether it is in earth or snow, pay strict attention to its shape. If your first impression is that the spoor drops down from the tip in a gentle, but almost immediate slope, and the pads appear to be fairly close together, it's a doe's track. Conversely, if you think the print is wide and angles out immediately at the tip with some space between the pads, you're looking at a buck's spoor.

It's also possible to tell an old buck from a young one, according to Carlson. "The older a buck gets, the more rounded the tops of the tracks become. They just plain wear down from constant contact with rocks, logs and other obstructions," he said.

There are also clues in the tracks as to the size of a buck. Heavier bucks always leave a deeper track, but you have to be careful not to be fooled by tracks over soft ground such as creek beds, moist gravel or organic material. If the dew claws don't appear in snow two inches or deeper, or you are probably looking at the print of an adolescent animal.

There are more clues to the sex of the deer that left the track. For starters, bucks usually drag their feet when travelling at an undisturbed, casual pace. Does, on the other hand, pick up their feet and almost prance atop the ground. Also, there are differences in the trails they leave. Bucks, especially those with large racks, tend to go over and around obstructions such as fallen logs and isolated thickets. Does are likely to do the opposite, crawling under the obstructions and weaving through the thickets.

Their line of travel is generally different and can often by conclusively ascertained. If the tracks take short, direct routes from one geographic area to another, they likely belong to a buck—especially if they are solitary tracks cutting through the woods. Does seem to meander—almost aimlessly at times. And they travel in groups much more often.

If there is snow on the ground, pay close attention to urine deposits along the trail. They are a dead giveaway. A doe's urine patch is a larger splotch on the snow, with an irregular pattern; a buck's urination is a more precise perforation of the snow. And if you spot orange or reddish-stained urine, you could have a doe in season, and that's almost as good as the buck himself.

Another trick is to carefully study the tracks surrounding a scrape. Because both bucks and does traffic the surrounding and immediate area, you can't take it for granted that all tracks leading directly from the scrape are a buck's. You'll just have to look for more clues, keeping the above pointers in mind. The key is to take it all slow.

More Lessons In Successful Trailing

The previous night Carlson had told me how important it was to "read" the tracks and make the correct interpretation of what the buck was doing. It sounded so simple. When the buck ran, we were going to run. When it slowed down, we were to do the same. Finally, when the buck left signs that it was about to bed down, we would circle to sneak up on it from an unsuspected angle.

I remember the anxiety I had about the prospects of having to make a good shot at running an animal.

Noble said I shouldn't worry. "Of all the bucks I've tracked down," he told me, "more than 90 percent never saw me or knew what had hit them."

Another fear I had was the one that must plague all hunters who give tracking even a feeble try: How do you know if the deer is a mile away or just over the next hill?

"You can boil it all down to two things," he began. "First, when that buck is on a runway, he's moving, looking for company, a doe in heat. Otherwise he'd be off on his own, looking for a safe place to feed or bed down.

"So when he's on a trail, you gotta work to keep up with him. And you can't keep up if you're worrying about being quiet. Besides, he's going to be way up ahead, and would probably associate any noise on the trail, at this point, with that of another deer.

"And second, when his tracks start meandering, splitting off the side here, straying over there, you know he's slowed way down. When you get to tracks like these, you can't make a sound and you can't be on the trail, either. If you are, you're dead, because he'll be spending more time watching his back trail than watching where he's going.

Suddenly, it all began to click for me. We had jogged across the runway and slowed down when we saw the buck's track splinter off the main trail. We were just about to get off the tracks when we spooked the buck.

Many hunters are proficient at getting on fresh tracks, but the reason most fail, from Noble's point of view, is that we don't know how to handle what he calls the "end-around."

"When I told you I'd teach you how to track up a buck, you probably had it in your head that we were going to sneak up on a deer in its track. That's how everyone thinks it's done. But I hardly ever walk up to a buck from his trail. They're too busy watching it. The trick is to dodge around and up ahead when you see him monkeying around, feeding or looking for a place to be down."

The bucks Noble hunts are some of the biggest bodied whitetails in North America, averaging 225 pounds, field-dressed. Northern Minnesota deer have to be big and tough or they won't survive the harsh winters.

We stayed on the trail for 100 yards before the tracks tightened up again. "See here," Noble whispered. "This is a good sign. Notice how he is already starting to slow down? He couldn't have winded us."

The buck carved a trail along a creek bed. We found where he had made a fresh rub, then waltzed right down the middle of a clearing.

"What are we going to do now?" Noble asked.

He was setting me up. "Well, we gotta keep up, don't we?" I asked.

"Not necessarily." Noble bent down and drew a diagram in the snow, showing how bucks pause on the opposite end of an opening and watch their back-trail. "They do it all the time, especially when they're headed into the wind. Every time a buck pulls this on you there's one thing to do. Circle around the opening. Sometimes he'll be there, sometimes he'll continue on."

It took a long time to skirt the edge. Sure enough, the buck was nowhere to be found. But Noble was dead on. Tracks told the story of a buck pausing in two places on the inside edge of the opening.

The trail continued. We circled around the open stuff and sneaked through the thickets. When the buck's tracks started circling back, Noble quickly changed course with me on his heels. We made a wide arc in the opposite direction of the buck's circle. Without any warning, the buck had checked his back-trail.

Noble wears felt liners inside zippered rubber overshoes so he can feel the landscape underfoot, avoid setting his weight in the wrong places and nimbly roll forward as he walks.

We picked up the track again at the edge of a small meadow. We had crossed some older tracks. Fortunately, Noble had learned how to differentiate a buck's track from a doe's, and how to distinguish one buck track from another.

To me, they all looked alike. Sure there were big, medium and small ones. And I was sure this method of looking at the tips, the width and the arch of the spoor was foolproof. But telling individual bucks apart?

"Your buck here isn't real old, but he's got pretty old, rounded hooves," he said. "Maybe a 5- or 6- year-old. Those others were only about 3 or 4 years old. They looked big, but their tips were much sharper and pointed. Besides, yours is missing a small chip out of his left hoof. I'm sure you couldn't have missed that!"

By now it was snowing. The tracks were beginning to fill in almost as fast as they were being made.

The season's first or second snowfall is Noble's favorite tracking situation. He says he can "just about ride their backs" under these conditions. First snow is his favorite for four reasons. First the deer haven't been pushed by wolves for seven or eight months. Second, they haven't been pushed by trackers for 10 months. Third, big bucks won't go very far once it starts snowing heavily, so Noble doesn't have to cover much ground. And fourth, the deer have forgotten that in the snow they don't blend as well with their surroundings, and they are apt to stand in fairly open places.

"If a guy isn't tracking then," Carlson says, "he's missing the closest thing he'll get to a sure buck."

The snow was getting so deep it was hard to tell which way the buck was heading. Noble explained an easy way to tell: "See these little tufts of snow? They're kicked up by the buck's hooves after he lifts them up and out of the snow. In deep snow, they always point in the direction the buck is heading."

When we reached a small stream, I noticed how the skim ice was broken by the buck's fresh track. I pointed proudly to my discovery and immediately Noble wrenched my head with his left hand. A growl grew in his throat. But it was too late.

Determination and Patience Pay Off

The fresh bed, 60 yards away, meant one thing; we had spooked the buck again. Ordinarily, the buck will give you a warning before he beds down, Noble said. He'll skip from one spot to another, turning around while scenting and gazing over his back-trail. This time he hadn't.

"I saw it coming," Noble said. "When it snows heavy like this, sometimes they just bed away."

The sun was less than an hour from setting, so it was too late to look for another track. Because he had tracked in this area for many years, Noble knew where the buck might be headed—a knoll at the tip of a large tag alder swamp. It was the perfect place for a buck under hot pursuit to hide out. Any predator would announce its presence when it broke through the swamp ice, and the buck could lie nearer the edge, winding the other side.

But if we could get there first. ...

We took the side of the swamp opposite the buck and were squeezing around the other edge when we picked up the buck's trail. I thought I saw where another deer had joined in from the west. Instead of continuing ahead or making a circle. Noble whirled around to the west with his gun up.

"Are you going to take him, or should I?" Noble whispered.

I looked to the west and saw the buck standing with its nose up and ears back. He was looking over the trail he had just made. I don't remember pulling the trigger, much less taking aim, but the gun went off. The bullet pulped both lungs.

The buck's neck was swollen with rut, and the base of his 10-point rack was as thick as my wrist. Noble flipped him over and brushed the snow off his front hooves. "Here's your buck," he said with pride. "See the chip in the hoof?"

I saw it and a whole lot more!

6

Ten Steps To Becoming
A Better Bowhunter

by Chuck Adams

*E*very bowhunter can improve. Hunting with archery gear is a complex game—a lot like playing chess. Even a chess master continues to learn new moves, and even an excellent bowhunter continues to polish his hunting and shooting skills.

Whether you have beginning, intermediate or advanced ability with a hunting bow, here are 10 steps guaranteed to improve your effectiveness afield.

1. Use Appropriate Shooting Gear

It's amazing how much mismatched shooting equipment gets carted into the woods. Bow and arrow must obviously match for decent, well-tuned accuracy. But more subtle factors can also influence your shooting ability.

The average bowhunter uses a compound bow with a draw length one or two inches too long. You are better off facing the target slightly as you aim, which shortens draw length and moves the bowstring away from your chest and forearm. If the string is within ½-inch of your chest clothing as you aim, your draw length is too long. Accuracy will suffer.

Similarly, most male bowhunters draw a bow five pounds too heavy. A 65-pound deer bow might feel easy on the backyard range, but try that same bow on a big buck from a cold tree stand. Nerves and cool weather can cause wobbling archery muscles unless you back down draw weight to compensate.

Many hunting archers select the wrong sort of compound wheel to match their shooting style. If you prefer a finger release, you need a round wheel or energy wheel. If you use a mechanical string release, a soft cam is better. Hard speed cams can be great for target shooting, but raise heck with broadhead flight.

Appropriate arrows for hunting seldom weigh less than 400 grains. The average male bowhunter after white-tailed deer is better served with arrows weighing 475 to 550 grains. These will fly better with broadheads, and create less game-spooking bow noise.

2. Become A Versatile Archery Shot

Target practice on bull's-eyes is great. Shooting at foam animal targets is even better. But the very best bowhunters go far beyond these two dimensions. They also shoot video target games like the Dart System, rove and practice-shoot at natural field targets like stumps and grass clumps, and bowhunt small game like rabbits, woodchucks, and squirrels.

Some serious downward shooting from a flat rooftop or tree stand is also essential to round out your field ability.

Such variety of practice eliminates shooting surprises on bowhunts for big game.

Most bowhunters of my acquaintance do not practice long enough or hard enough before deer season begins. Among the worst offenders can be long-time, somewhat cocky bowhunters who might be prone to tell you they know it all.

No matter who you are, shooting more is bound to help. Shooting year-round is ideal, but shooting three or four months prior to deer season is an absolute must. It takes time to condition bow-shooting muscles, time to train your mind and body to work in harmony, and time to develop versatility on bull's-eyes, animal targets, video targets, and small game.

The best bowhunters shoot slow—never fast. They launch an arrow, and then give their body a minute or so of rest while they analyze what they did right or wrong. Similarly, competent archers seldom shoot every day. Like weight lifters, they work out every other day at most, and never practice after muscles become tired, painful, or unsteady.

3. Silence And Camouflage Your Tackle

A noisy bow scares the dickens out of skittish game like white-tailed deer. Studies of slow-motion deer-shooting video have proven that close-range bucks can easily hear and duck a fast but noisy bow/arrow combination. It's better to have a slower, quieter bow.

In situations where you know the shooting range—like from a tree stand for deer—a moderately heavy arrow of 500 to 525 grains will absorb nasty noise-making vibration. Remaining bow noise can be stifled with a rubber or hydraulic stabilizer plus commercial string and cable silencers.

Be sure bow add-ons like sight and quiver are tightly affixed, because one loose connection can buzz like a hopping-mad rattlesnake.

Shooting gear must be non-glare and medium-colored to blend with the woods. Fortunately, most bow companies sell models with effective camo patterns. The best aluminum arrows are dull-anodized in woodsy colors to avoid the eyes of game.

A surprising percentage of bows, arrows, and accessories have practical camo patterns but alarmingly shiny surfaces. If shooting hardware reflects light, it will signal danger to game.

4. Assemble Key Hunting Accessories

Many modern archers rely too heavily on gimmicks for success. They enter the woods draped like a Christmas tree with the latest, hottest bowhunting "aids."

Smart bowhunters assemble a lean, mean hunting accessory kit. Rangefinder, knife, binocular, survival gear, scent products, game calls, and other key items fit neatly in a small day pack, fanny pack, or two pants pockets. Everybody's hunting-accessory kit is different, because everybody's hunting needs are unique, but effective bowhunters keep gadgets to a minimum.

Too much gear can impede easy, silent movement. It can also ruin swift, effective shooting. If any hunting gadget has doubtful use, leave it at home. It will probably get in your way.

5. Research Habitat and Scout With Care

You should bowhunt where animals hang out. This seems silly to say, but many archers waste days and weeks of precious vacation time in low-percentage game areas.

Study current record lists from Pope & Young, Boone & Crockett, and Safari Club International. Call state game department offices and talk to head biologists. Contact the local game warden. Talk to taxidermists in areas you wish to hunt. All these ploys will tell you where and where not to find lots of animals or stand-out trophy heads.

Once you narrow your hunting area, allot time to scout for trails, tracks, droppings, beds, rubs, scrapes and animals themselves. Try to anticipate what other bowhunters will do, so you can bowhunt where archery pressure is light.

If you bowhunt an expert-recommended area, and pinpoint your focus in remote or overlooked pockets with lots of animal activity, you will increase your hunting odds tenfold.

6. Plot Creative Hunting Strategies

Modern day trophy deer did not grow up by being naive. Such animals usually control the hunting situation.

Thinking hunters can turn the tables on wary game. It pays to study other bowhunters in your hunting area. You can bet the animals have! For example, 9 out of 10 deer hunters sit in tree stands within half a mile of roads. This means that you should walk in a mile, or try a ground blind in a treeless place.

If you are hunting on public land, don't toot on your grunt tube repeatedly like every other bozo in the region. Slip around silently, and catch call-shy bucks off guard.

Similarly, a good stand hunter switches ambush sites every day or two. He keeps animals off balance, and never leaves loads of human scent around one favorite tree stand or ground blind.

Creative strategies are necessary to surprise animals wise to the standard, predictable ways of hunters.

7. Learn How Your Bow Works

The average compound bow without accessories has 50 to 55 separate, distinct parts. These combine to produce a relatively trouble-free product. But bow parts occasionally break, wear, warp or otherwise fail to function properly.

Similarly, bow tuning can be a touchy thing. If an arrow rest slips, nocking point slides or synthetic cable stretches, your bow won't shoot well anymore.

For these reasons, every hunter should intimately understand his bow. If you know how your "string gun" works, you will know what to do when it doesn't. It's as simple as that.

If your archery dealer will agree to help, have him completely disassemble your hunting bow while you watch. Learn to work on the setup yourself, the same as a soldier learns to field-strip his weapon. And learn to tune your bow to perfection by reading archery books and consulting your archery dealer.

It's worth paying an archery store technician $25 or $50 for this sort of help, plus some tips on what might go wrong with your particular bow and what the field cures might be. If you are familiar with your shooting tool, you can carry some common-sense repair tools and replacement parts in case something breaks or drifts out of tune in the field.

8. Persist No Matter What

Good bowhunters are like bulldogs. Once they grab hold of a challenge, they never let go.

More than any other factor, persistence gets the game. Archery hunting is typically a series of maybes, might-haves, and near misses at success. But stick-to-itiveness usually pays off in the long run. Sooner or later, all those frustrating failures will evaporate in one moment of perfect hunting, straight shooting and old-fashioned good luck.

Even the best bowhunters blow stalks, take stands in the wrong place, and miss shots. Don't let them tell you otherwise. The difference between "the men and the boys" is confidence to keep on trying day after day and week after week.

If you learn by your mistakes, and keep on hunting, bowhunting success will ultimately come your way!

9. Know When To And When Not To Shoot

Smart bowhunters recognize high-percentage, low-percentage, and no-percentage shots. They only take high-percentage opportunities.

Deer-shooting success requires five key things. First, the animal must be stationary and relaxed, with ears back and muscles at a slouch. Second, the animal must not be able to see you draw your bow. If you can see the critter's eye, it can probably see you move to shoot.

Third, the shot must be completely clear, with no bushes, tree limbs, or similar obstacles blocking the front half of the animal. Fourth, animal angle must be correct. You should only shoot at deer that are broadside or quartering slightly away.

And finally, keep shots within your personal sure-kill distance. Most bowhunters cannot consistently hit a buck's 8-inch vital chest beyond 25 or 30 yards.

Here's when not to shoot. Don't shoot at moving or keyed-up critters. These are likely to crouch or wheel before the arrow arrives.

Don't draw in an animal's face. Even a broadside deer can easily see you draw. Don't try to "sneak" an arrow through foliage. This never works. Don't shoot at a deer's frontal chest, butt, head, neck or other marginal areas. Wait for the large chest target provided by a broadside or slightly quartering deer.

10. Keep Ethics Foremost In Mind

Bowhunters owe it to the animals and to themselves to take only high-percentage, sure-kill shots. Furthermore, archers should bend over backwards to obey all game laws and treat private and public hunting property with respect. Anti-hunters are poised to pounce on any public display of hunter misconduct, be it a crippled animal staggering around, a messy campsite left behind, or a hunting-law violation written up in the local newspaper.

If we want to enjoy our great sport into the next century, we must all act like professionals in the field!

7

The Masters' Secrets
Of Deer Calling

by John E. Phillips

Calling is a relatively recent innovation in the stew of techniques and tactics that are deer hunting. Although many hunters have seen phenomenal results when they've used deer calls, others have been disappointed. Remember, calling deer is another tool to be added to your list of hunting aids. No hunting aid always works all the time, but some hunting aids will be productive some of the time.

Calling deer often pays off in buck dividends because deer are very social animals. They have a distinct pecking order, and they communicate all year long. The wise hunter will learn the language of the whitetails, understand what the deer are saying and use that knowledge to call deer. As with any hunting aid, the masters of the sport utilize special tactics to make deer calls more effective. Here are some calling tips from the pros to improve your odds for taking a buck this season.

Dick Kirby, Quaker Boy Calls

One of the biggest mistakes in deer calling is some hunters rely on their calls instead of using good, sound hunting tactics. The deer call is a hunting aid. Before you can use it effectively to pull bucks to you, you have to be conscious of not making woodsmanship mistakes that run bucks away from you.

The deer call does not supersede the buck's ability to smell human odor nor his ability to see the human form. A deer call will pull a buck into an area where you can take him only if he can't smell you. You can't disregard the wind when using a deer call. To get the maximum effectiveness out of your deer call, make sure you first scout the area, know which direction the deer should come from, and sit downwind of the deer before you start calling.

If you hunt with a favorable wind so the deer can't smell you, and sit still to keep the deer from seeing you, then when you do call, you'll increase the effectiveness of your calling by 100 percent.

Wil Primos, Primos Game Calls

When the rattling bag, which simulates the clashing of antlers, first came on the market, I thought the idea was a joke. But now I manufacture one that I've learned to use very effectively with my deer calling.

Observe bucks as soon as they come out of the velvet. Notice that from time to time they clash antlers—not actually fighting but sparring in a playful manner by merely touching antlers. Then usually each of them will give a soft, light grunt, which other deer will come to investigate when they hear it.

A combination of light grunting and light rattling seems to be the most productive during the opening week of bow season, before the deer have been disturbed.

I believe one of the most critical keys to successful deer calling is to understand deer will come to almost any sound produced by other deer. Instead of trying to complicate deer calling and worrying about what type of grunt you should or shouldn't be giving, remember deer will come to you if you can make noises like a deer.

Deer calling also works because deer in an area know each other. When you give a deer call, you're imitating the sound a new deer makes. Deer will want to come and meet that new deer in the territory.

A problem I often encounter when a buck is in close is how to give a call without moving so the deer won't see me. I've designed a small call, the Still Grunter, about the size of my thumb, that fits inside my mouth and duplicate the sound of a larger grunt, but is a hands-free option that keeps me still.

Brad Harris, Lohman Manufacturing

I'm convinced the volume, not the tone you use when you blow a deer call, often determines the success or failure you'll have with any deer call. Most people try to call too loudly and aggressively. The amount of wind, the terrain and the distance you are from the animal help you to decide the volume to use to call a deer. If you're attempting to reach a deer 150 yards away with your call, and the wind is blowing, then you need to blow that call loudly for the deer to hear it. But if the deer is only 80 yards from you, and little or no wind is present, then reduce the volume of your calling so the deer barely can hear it at that distance.

If you're blind calling without a deer in sight or knowledge of where the deer is, make soft calls first that probably only can be heard from 40 to 50 yards away. If you can see 80 to 90 yards, but don't spot a deer, next call loudly enough for your call to reach that far. Then pick up the volume to let the call reach out further to attempt to attract deer at greater distances.

On a calm, still day in flat, open terrain, I've seen deer come to a call 200 yards away, but if you're hunting rolling terrain on a windy day, your call only may be effective for 75 yards or less. Deer calling usually is most productive at a range from 80 to 100 yards.

When a bowhunter sees a buck out of range of his bow, he can pull that buck to within bow range. The gun hunter who is trying to bag a buck in thick cover often can pull that buck out of the cover into an open area where he can shoot, if he'll use a deer call. Remember, less calling is better calling.

Terry Rohm, Wellington Outdoors

Deer calling is much like turkey calling. When you call a turkey in that's looking right at you, you don't make another call, because the bird may pinpoint your location. If a gobbler stares straight at the spot where a hen is supposed to be but doesn't see her, he'll leave the area.

Deer are just as cautious once they arrive at the place where another deer is supposed to be calling. If they don't see the deer making the sound, they generally will become nervous and leave the region. If a deer is coming to you, don't call!

When I can see a deer I want to call to, I attempt to throw the sound of my call down toward the ground behind me—just as I do when a tom is in close. I want the deer to think the sound is coming from the ground and just past the spot where I have my stand. By throwing the call behind you, the deer will come in closer to your stand to search for the deer behind you instead of expecting to see a deer in front of you.

To bring deer in closer when you're giving grunts like a buck or using rattling antlers, use some type of buck lure. Or if you're giving doe calls, put out some type of doe lure. A buck wants to confirm with either his eyes or his nose what his ears are telling him. Deer will come to a hunting aid that appeals to one of their senses. However, you greatly increase the odds of the deer's coming to you when you use a combination of hunting aids that appeal to several of the deer's senses.

Ron Haydel, Haydel's Game Calls

Rather than sounding like one deer, I try to sound like two deer in the same place at the same time by mixing up my calling. I'll give two short grunts to sound like one deer and next give a long grunt and flare my hand at the end of the call to change the pitch and the tone to sound like a dominant buck. Then I make another short grunt at the end of the sequence to sound like a subordinate buck.

Our company has developed the Variable Tone Call, which resembles our duck calls with a hole in the bottom. By covering the hole, you'll be able to give the sound of one deer grunting. By uncovering the hole, you'll sound like a different deer. You also can vary the sound you get from a call by changing your hand position on the end of the call.

Another trick I've learned to use after the rut and sometimes during the rut is to give either a short, tending grunt or a bleat call. Perhaps bucks get beat up so much during the rut that when breeding season is over, they're more likely to come to a bleat call that doesn't indicate aggression or a tending grunt call than they are to rattling antlers or a dominant, aggressive grunt call. If that buck has been fighting for a week or two, the last thing he will want to look for is another fight.

Jerry Peterson, Woods Wise Products

Common sense tells you that if a buck has the option of going to a buck call, two bucks fighting or a doe call, the buck will respond to the doe call. The doe is what creates the fighting and the aggression in the bucks. The dominance order bucks set up is to determine which one gets to breed the does. So utilize a call that sounds like a doe, which has a higher-pitched grunt than bucks. Also, a doe ready to breed often gives the bleat call, which is why I think the bleat call is one of the most effective calls for a buck hunter.

A bleat call will draw in any buck in an area. If you give a dominant buck grunt call with aggressive sounding grunts, you may run off all the bucks in the region. Also the dominant buck may or may not be able to hear your calling. I'm convinced a buck will choose meeting a ready-to-breed female before he'll go to do battle.

Another reason I believe doe calling is more effective than buck calling is because a fawn learns as soon as it is born that the soft, grunting of his mother means, "Come here." I believe a deer, whether buck or doe, always associates the soft grunting of the doe to mean, "Come here."

Wayne Carlton, Carlton's Calls & Hunting Stuff

When bucks are chasing does during the rut or when bucks are running to a fight, they often will grunt while running. As their lungs and internal organs bounce, they give off a shaky, broken-type grunt like humans make when they're running and grunting.

I've been able to use this running grunt call to cause bucks to stop, wheel around and come running to me. This bouncing grunt will cause deer to come in quicker and/or also will stop deer walking away from where you are and make them turn around and charge toward your hunting site.

Another tactic is to vary the sound of the call by collapsing or extending the tube on the end of a grunt call to sound as though several deer are in the same area. Compressing the tube gives off a high-pitched grunt like a doe's or a younger buck's call, and extending the tube makes a deeper, low-pitched call like an older, dominant buck. Between those two extremes, you can either slightly compress or extend the tube and change the tonal quality of the call. Altering the tone of your call means you can call more.

Most experts recommend calling only every 15 minutes. However, a buck can move in and out of the hearing range of your call during the 15 minutes when you weren't calling. Changing the tonal quality of your call allows you to call every three to five minutes, sound like a different deer each time you call and increases your odds by 200 to 300 percent for calling in a deer.

Harold Knight, Knight & Hale Game Calls

One of the big mistakes hunters make in calling deer is to believe one call always will work on any deer and that deer calling is the only tactic to use. When I'm selecting a deer call, I want one I can blow loud enough to reach far away deer and one I can blow soft and low to call in close-by deer.

I believe deer calls are most effective on calm, still days when the deer can hear them, and I'm also convinced soft calls will bring in more deer than loud calls will. No matter how much volume you put through your deer call, make sure the last call you give is a low, soft, subtle call. Use a deer call to grab the buck's attention and let him know another deer is in the area, but then the call needs to be subtle enough so the buck can't pinpoint exactly where that other deer is. Since deer generally grunt very, very softly, if you grunt too loudly and too much, you'll call the deer, and he'll spot you.

A call I've learned is very deadly when hunting deer in the rut is the Hyperventilator Call. When a buck is running a doe, he wheezes and grunts at the same time. When he blows out, he often will be grunting, and when he sucks air in, usually he will be wheezing. I believe this wheeze/grunt sound a buck makes when chasing a doe is one of the strongest calls you can use, because any other buck in the region recognizes that sound and believes an estrus doe is close by. He'll come to that call in hopes of getting to the estrus doe first.

8

Early Season Feeding Frenzy

by Jim Casada

*M*ention mast to the average deer hunter, and immediately his thoughts turn to acorns. There is no denying the importance of oak mast, but acorns are not necessarily the food item of first choice for deer in the fall. Indeed, where they are available, several of the foodstuffs collectively referred to as "soft mast" take first place on a whitetail's dinner plate.

Perhaps the first point to be made about soft mast is that it will be crucial to your hunting strategy only if available when the hunting season is open. Since the soft mast availability varies greatly depending on where you live and hunt, as well as with the individual mast item, it is a consideration to keep in mind before you begin tactical planning on stand placement.

Deer Candy

A good place to start when it comes to soft mast is with the various fruits that hunters sometimes refer to as "deer candy." Anywhere there are deer and bearing autumn fruit trees, the deer will quickly zero in on the ripening and falling apples and pears. Find a consistently productive apple or pear tree on an abandoned farm or in a remote pasture and you'll have a prize hunting spot.

Pears are a bit more predictable in bearing fruit thanks to hardiness and less likelihood of a late frost killing the blooms, so they are more consistent year after year. These fruits virtually guarantee a feeding frenzy at ripening time, and if that comes during a period when you can hunt, you'll be wise to take advantage of the opportunity.

Indeed, some shrewd hunters I know go a step further and actively "cultivate" the fruit trees when they find them. It's a good idea to keep other vegetation cleared away from apples and pears and perhaps even do a bit of pruning in late winter to enhance fruit production next year. (Be sure to check the regulations on baiting in your state and follow the requirements.) In some cases state game departments have planted fruit trees on public hunting lands or they maintain existing trees.

As the fruits start dropping, deer will make daily feeding trips to enjoy the juicy offerings. On many occasions I've seen deer stand on their back legs to reach an apple still dangling on the tree. In some areas apples and pears have come and gone before the season is open, but in others you can enjoy several weeks of bow or gun hunting near fruit trees. Some varieties of apples cling stubbornly to limbs, not falling until long after all leaves are gone. If you know of such a tree, it can be a great place to hunt on the day following a storm or strong winds. Deer seem to have a knack of knowing that the foul weather will have knocked delicious fruit tidbits to the ground.

Another early season delight for deer is wild grapes and their close kin, scuppernongs and muscadines. In one form or another these are widespread across much of the country, and a lot of varieties of wild grapes ripen in early fall. When they do, deer are greatly attracted to them, and for bowhunters they can be quite important.

The grape season is a fairly short one, because usually they ripen and are gone in a period of only two or three weeks. For that brief time span, however, they constitute an important item in a deer's diet. This is especially true over the Southeast, where wild grapes are found almost anywhere there are woods, overgrown fields, fence rows, or any type of uncultivated land. Deer seem particularly drawn to the big, individual growing grapes known as scuppernongs and muscadines. Often, scouting expeditions to old, abandoned farms or homesteads will reveal fruit trees and an arbor or two of thriving vines (a grape vine can live for a century or more). No matter what location you're in, preseason scouting should include keeping an eye open for grape vines. If they drop fruit during the hunting season, be there.

As attractive as apples, pears and wild grapes can be in places where they are available, they take a distinct second place to another fruit of the land. For deer, the most widespread and appealing of all the fruity candies is the persimmon. A hardy resident of fence rows, overgrown fields and abandoned farmsteads, the persimmon produces small orange-colored globes, often in great abundance, that deer dearly love. Better still, persimmons usually are at their sweetest when hunting season deer activity is at the peak.

Contrary to popular folk wisdom, it is not true that persimmons are inedible until after the first frost. It is usually late October or into November, at the peak of the rut in many hunting areas, before persimmons become sweet. Until the point when they ripen, though, many a city lad visiting country cousins has learned persimmons have a tartness that gives new meaning to "pucker power." Unlike humans, deer somehow know (probably through smell) when persimmons are ready to eat. And once that happens, they gather at bearing trees as if addicted.

Fortunately, ripe persimmons are slow to fall, in some cases clinging to limbs long after they have matured. As a result, you might be able to hunt this soft mast over a period of several weeks. However, such is not likely to be the case if the fruits are discovered by opossums, skunks or raccoons. These critters and many others love the tasty treats. For that matter, so do humans. If you've have ever been privileged to feast on a properly prepared persimmon pudding, you'll understand why. It is a country-boy gourmet's delight.

Deer hunters owe it to themselves to locate every persimmon tree in the areas they regularly hunt and check them before the season to see if they are bearing mast. If so, make plans to hunt them at the appropriate time. Thanks to the fact that their ripening coincides so closely with the open deer hunting season across wide areas of the country, not to mention just how much deer love the fruit, persimmons deserve more attention than they are sometimes given. They are deer candy at its sweetest, and even the wisest of old bucks is likely to have a sweet tooth.

Take note that many scent manufacturers have recognized the importance of soft mast as an attractant for hungry deer. Examples of the aforementioned soft mast fruits can be purchased as an attractant scent. If you buy and try one, follow the directions and let the deer be the final judge.

More Mast

In addition, there are a number of other soft mast items that deserve attention. Among the foods that are noteworthy include: sumac berries, French mulberries (also known as American beauty berry), Osage orange fruits (the tree is known in some areas as bodock), Maypops (wild passion fruit), paw-paws, and the fruit of the honey locust.

Sumac is easily identified in early fall because of the vivid scarlet of its leaves, and the red clusters of berries are also readily visible. It is my personal opinion that deer find several other types of soft mast preferable to sumac, but they eat it regularly. Also, sumac seems to bear every year, a quality that is not true of many other varieties of soft mast. So do French mulberries, which are easily spotted thanks to their vivid pinkish-purple color. Whitetails eat the berries of this low-growing plant and also find the tips of its limbs quite desirable.

The Osage orange bears a huge rough-skinned, round, baseball-sized fruit, and deer often will nibble on them when they are available. As with sumac, though, it does not seem to be a preferred food item. Much the same is true of passion fruit, although deer will break open the yellow balls of this ground vine to get at the pulp inside.

On the other hand, when it comes to paw-paws, a musky tasting fruit with something of a resemblance to the smell and taste of a banana, deer love them. Unfortunately, paw-paws are rather rare, being found mostly in rich ground where there is plenty of moisture. However, if you can identify the fruit and know where several plants are located, rest assured deer know that location also.

Honey Locust Honeyhole

To me, the pods of the honey locust might be the most overlooked of all the types of soft mast. They grow on the variety of locust that is adorned with the long, sharp thorns dreaded by hunters. Once leaves have fallen, the brown leathery pods are easily spotted. They normally do not begin dropping until well into November. It seems they offer deer a sweet treat when most similar items are no longer available. Just pick up a recently fallen locust pod and peel away the covering to get at the fleshy area around the seeds. One taste will tell you why the word "honey" goes with this species of locust. It will also explain why old-timers sometimes brewed a sweet-tasting beer from the pods.

Deer dine on the seed pods daintily, munching only the portion that's meaty, and when they are through the leftovers are somewhat reminiscent of the rinds remaining after a summertime watermelon feast. Honey locust trees are often found standing alone, and if you have one covered with pods, it's a fine place to be hunting when they begin to fall.

No matter where you live in whitetail land, it's likely that one or more of the soft mast bushes, vines and trees noted above are present. Because of that, it's important to learn how to identify these important deer foods. Once you have the ability to identify the various types of vegetative delights, you can then plan your hunting strategy accordingly.

Soft mast is almost never as abundant as hard mast, but the fact that many types are particularly appealing to deer makes it important, especially early in the season. The sweetness of the fruits makes them a definite favorite of deer that are loading up for the long winter ahead. Plan your early season hunts with these considerations in mind and your deer hunting season will end quickly. Then you might have the rest of the fall to hunt all those other game species you've been dreaming about.

9

Breaking The Ice

by Judd Cooney

*L*ooking for a way to break the ice on that first bow-killed buck? Then get out in the woods and kill the first doe that gives you the opportunity. That's right, a doe!

Every year I get bowhunters wanting to book a hunt with me who are primarily interested in antelope, mule deer or elk. It's easy to identify the beginning bowhunters, because they usually have their sights set on a real trophy buck or bull.

When I get to questioning them on the species they have taken with a bow and their trophy qualities, it more often than not turns out that they have never taken a trophy animal of any kind. In many cases they have yet to take a big game animal with a bow and arrow, but they want to book a hunt with a guide or outfitter because they feel that will increase their chances of killing a trophy animal.

Now don't get me wrong. By booking with a legitimate guide or outfitter they should have a better opportunity to get a shot at a good animal, but the final outcome of that shot is going to depend entirely on the bowhunter.

I would hate to count the number of times I have had a beginning bowhunter within range of a trophy animal and had him blow the shot, simply because he didn't have the experience or the control to put the arrow in the right place at the right time.

I don't hesitate to tell my beginning clients that trophy hunting is great for the first few days, but if they have never taken one of the animals they are hunting with a bow, they should do so on the hunt regardless of size or gender.

There is no question in my mind that once a bowhunter takes the first animal of a species his mental attitude is totally different on the next hunt for that species. There is no longer that nagging little doubt about whether or not he can actually harvest an animal of the species with his bow. The mental pressure is off and he knows he can do the job on a good trophy, given the chance.

This mental change makes all the difference in the world when that trophy white-tailed buck comes meandering through the woods or brush toward your tree stand or blind.

Once a bowhunter has taken one or more does and decides he is going to get that first buck, it then takes patience, perseverance and hard work. First of all, you have to decide for yourself just how bad you want that first buck. Chances are, you are going to put your willpower and patience to the supreme test by passing all the does that come within range to get a shot at a buck.

The perseverance comes when you keep going out time after time and stay with the hunt until you are successful on that first buck. It is not easy to sit, day after day, and not take a shot. Each time you pass a shot you're going to wonder if maybe that was the last chance you're going to get that season. As the days pass you're going to find it harder and harder to pass does and hold out for a buck. The only way you are going to succeed is by staying mentally tough and confident right up until the last minute of daylight on the last day of the season.

Holding out for a buck is giving yourself an extra challenge but you should also be realistic. If you and your family like venison, give yourself a final chance to fill your tag with a doe before the season ends. Our family has lived on game meat for years and each fall I like to challenge myself by trophy hunting until the last couple of days of the season. If I haven't found a trophy to my liking by that time, or even worse have missed a trophy animal, then I simply hunt for a legal animal to supply meat for our table and wait for the next season to trophy hunt again.

There have been numerous times when I have waited until the last day to fill my tag and then found myself outsmarted by the female of the species and gone home "skunked." Even when this happens I figure I am ahead of the game because I learn something new and different on each hunt and outing, which makes me a better bowhunter the next season. Each animal taken gives you that much more experience and confidence.

All the foregoing may add to your chances of success on that first buck but the real key to your success is going to boil down to one element, hard work! The saying, "being lucky is 99 percent the result of hard work," couldn't be more true when it comes to breaking the ice on that first buck. The larger the buck you set your sights for, the harder you are going to have to work.

Start your work long before the season by locating areas where there are good populations of deer. This can be done by contacting local game and fish officers. Try to locate areas with maximum deer densities. Once you get this information, then contact local sportsmen, farmers, sporting goods store owners and local law enforcement officers. The highway patrol and sheriff's deputies spend a lot of time driving the roads and just may be able to put you onto a good area here they have seen bucks. This phase of your hunt is most important and by using the best public relations skills you can muster, you may find a "honeyhole" that will produce your first buck.

Once you locate an area with a good deer population, spend as much time as you can scouting the area. At first this is best done by glassing in the early morning and late evening to get some idea of deer movements and possibly locating a shootable buck. The next step is serious "on the ground" scouting to locate primary feeding and bedding areas. This is easily done if you are hunting along the edges of corn fields, alfalfa fields, orchards or other areas where deer feed regularly.

If you will be hunting areas where the deer move around a lot and there are no well-defined feeding areas your task is a bit more difficult. Spend your time glassing creek bottoms, brush patches, woody draws and such. Don't ignore small areas of cover such as a small, cattail-filled slough, weedy fence lines or a small willow thicket. Often, deer will sneak into such areas before daylight and spend all day bedded there. These places are often out in the open and so obvious that nobody would expect a deer to be anywhere near.

Always expect the unexpected from deer and don't ever take it for granted that a deer wouldn't use an area because it is too small or too close to a building or road. These spots are bonus areas and are usually tough to hunt. But when deer disappear from their normal areas of feeding and bedding, especially after the gun opener, keep these spots in mind because you just might find a wise old buck using one of them on a regular basis.

The best place to ambush a deer is along a well-defined trail leading from heavy cover to a feeding area. Locate as many of these trails as you can during your early scouting. Then concentrate on the ones that show the most use. During the rut, bucks will use these trails for their scrapes.

If your time is limited and you really want to monitor the activity on a particular trail or a scrape, there are several new trail monitoring devices on the market. This type of device can provide invaluable information on deer movements and allow you to pattern deer even though you are not on the spot yourself.

Try to find a blind location close enough to the heavy cover the deer are using during the day to catch them when they first come out. Be sure your blind is far enough away so you don't spook them when walking to your blind. By staying near the heavy cover, you will catch the deer moving early in the evening in good shooting light. During a morning hunt, you'll have a chance at them a little later in the morning as they move away from the feeding area to bed down for the day.

When placing your stand, regardless of whether it's a ground blind or tree stand, remember to pick a spot where you will have the predominant wind in your favor during the prime hunting hours. It's also a good idea to try and pick a spot where you will have the sun at your back.

When building your blind or putting up a tree stand, attempt to get a location where you have a dense background to keep from being silhouetted. Forget the fact that deer aren't supposed to look up because they darn sure will, and a head and shoulders outline against the sky or a thin background of brush either from a ground blind or tree stand will put them in high gear and ruin future chances for you from that location.

In areas where the deer are hunted exclusively out of tree stands, don't hesitate to put in a good ground blind or even a "pit blind" near a trail. I have been in many areas where deer have no conception of danger from ground level and yet will spook at the slightest movement or sound from above. Don't hesitate to put up several blinds at different locations so you can adapt to any change in the deer's patterns and move around from one to the other to keep from being patterned by the deer.

It's a good idea to do some "stand watching" immediately prior to the bow season to determine which stand is getting the most action around it. Don't sit in your hunting tree stand! Do your looking with binoculars or a spotting scope from a distance so there is no chance of the deer smelling or seeing you and associating danger with the area around your stand. If a deer ever gets spooked near your stand you can bet it won't come near that location again during hunting hours. This is especially true of bucks, which seem to be much more cautious and spooky than does.

Now comes the hard part: Be patient and wait for that buck to come within bow range. You have already taken a deer with your bow so you know you can accomplish the task, given the opportunity. Spend all the time you can in your blind and when the moment comes, you'll find it really isn't all that difficult to break the ice on that first buck.

10

Scrape Hunting Secrets

by Ron Doss

Whitetail Hunter finds a tub-sized scrape. It's under a thick-trunked cedar hooked bare of bark waist high. The limbs above the scrape are mangled and broken. The aromatic sap is still oozing. The newly overturned humus proves the scrape's freshness. Some still damp dirt clods lay 20 feet away from the scrape.

A deer track—no; two different sized tracks—are stamped in the bared, damp earth. The imprinted track edges are sharp and well-defined, not old enough to have weathered and softened.

Whitetail Hunter finds a tree downwind, 30 yards away from the scrape; the perfect spot to hang a tree stand. He is set up to take the dominant rutting buck in the area...or so he thinks!

When he found the scrape, overjoyed Whitetail Hunter, with adrenal glands pumping 110 percent, probably bent over and stuck his nose in the bared earth to sniff for urine scent. Sweat droplets ran down his nose, dripping to the ground. He scooped out a handful of dirt to break up and roll around in his bare hand, to smell more closely. He fingered the broken cedar limbs in awe of the rutting force that drove the buck into such a frenzy.

A doe, holed up nearby, was spooked by Whitetail Hunter's actions and bounded off in white-flagged annoyance. He scarcely noticed her, though her flag was more half mast than at full flight display.

She's not the big buck that made this scrape. He's Boone & Crockett for sure. His full shoulder mount will adorn Whitetail Hunter's fireplace, invoking "oooohs" and "aaaahs" from envious onlookers for years to come.

Whitetail Hunter will likely spend some long hours in his tree stand, watching this scrape until his eyes water. The surrounding tree trunks will sway and slither through his fatigue-induced eyestrain.

He may score from this setup. But the result will probably be a curious, immature buck sneakily checking for messages left by the absent dominant scrape-maker. Or the hunter may give in, abandon the image of the rocking chair rack mounted over his fireplace. Or he may opt for meat or to save face or to take a doe or button on the antlerless hunt.

This story could have gone the other way. It could have followed the track of his mental imagery, scoring on the 3½-plus-year-old mature buck. From the start, when he saw the scrape, the tell-tale damage to the cedar or even recognized an area likely to be used for rutting scrapes, he should have backed off. He should have treated the area with the same respect, or fear, as he would the den of two dozen timber rattlers!

When he was close enough to see the detail described, he was already too close. Chances are the dominant buck will never return to this scrape in daylight, if ever. If he does, he'll wait for the protective darkness of midnight to take care of his business. Or he may snort at the human "stink," and high tail it for the county line.

A pet 1½-year-old buck, properly licensed by the state of Mississippi to be a pet, has a pen all to himself. The enclosure was once a cattle feed-out lot, giving a sense of the area and space he inhabits. Though he's the dominant buck in his area, even if by default, he's never made a scrape. He has no contact with any other deer, only humans.

"Buckwheat" may be an exception to the millions of deer in the wild, but I suspect strongly from experience that scrape making is reactive. Until a buck's scraping instinct mechanism is triggered by contact with the opposite sex, he will not scrape. He will "hook" or "rub" trees, often licking them as Buckwheat does, depositing scent from his forehead, preorbital and oral glands on the visual displays of the hooked trees. Whether this triggers the pheromone release in does, which then triggers the buck's scrape making instinct, or some other natural stimulus triggers it, we face the proverbial chicken and egg. The point is that a buck with no doe contact will not make scrapes.

We've read of territorial scrapes, impulsive scrapes, line scrapes and even doe scrapes. There are, for our purposes, only two kinds of scrapes: active and inactive, or "live" ones and "dead" ones.

Whitetails are not territorial. That may come as a shock, but it is true. Bucks inhabit a preferred core area, usually selected when they are driven off by their estrus mothers to prevent inbreeding. This driving away of male offspring as they become sexually mature is a fact of deer behavior. If a second year fawn is seen in the company of a doe very long after August or September, you can bet your bottom dollar that the tag-along is a female. The males are long gone from the family setting by that time.

This core area is not, in the true sense, a "territory," to be defended against invaders. More than one mature buck often inhabits a favorable core area, even bedding down side-by-side. It is when the rutting urges start that they become isolationist and aggressive, but not over any territory. It all has to do with the proximity of a willing doe.

Impulsive scrapes, scrapes that appear to have been made for no known reason, have a definite purpose. Imagine a string of scrapes along a ridge, around the edges of a swamp, or following the meeting point of two or more different types of cover or terrain. Visualize them as a fisherman's trot line set with baited hooks every few feet the length of the line and fished until one or two of the hooks get enough bites to establish a pattern of catching fish. That is exactly what a string of scrapes is intended to do: "fish" for does.

Early on, the buck smells does, either through direct contact or second-hand, from tracks with residual interdigital scent or from spots where does have urinated or deposited fecal mass. That screams "doe" to his brain! This direct or indirect contact with does triggers the scrape-making instinct.

The buck, through this minimal contact, is able to determine from the minute scent residue the age, sex, general physical condition and the probable estrus onset of the doe or does. The scent kicks off his role in the annual reproductive cycle. He sets out his "line." Early in the season, he checks the line scrapes sporadically. The season progresses. His own internal functions and glandular secretions thicken his neck, broaden his nose and swell his tarsal glands. Now, he checks his scrape line more often for a "bite."

A doe begins to sense or "feel" the nearing onset of her estrus, and leaves a urinal or fecal message in one of the line scrapes. She may also rub her forehead gland on one of his nearby hooked trees, or lick the bared inner wood to reinforce the message. The buck checks his line, interprets the complicated messages and goes into frenzied activity.

He bares the ground, scraping and flinging the accumulated leaves and ground cover, digging his nose into the scent-soaked, bared earth to catch as much scent as possible. He will "phlemen" the scent by curling his lip to trap and concentrate the scent, then inhale it, forcing the scent deep into his nostrils. To him, it must be like an internasal shot of mating drug. It saturates his nasal membranes, going directly to the correct sensors in the buck's brain. He is in full rut. The line scrape is now an active rutting scrape.

Depending on the urgency of the doe's estrus onset, she may lie down nearby and wait for the buck to return and find her. When he does, she leads him on a merry chase, sometimes for several days. They may romp over miles, until she senses the exact moment that copulation will accomplish conception.

The buck may stay with her after this first act for another few hours, insuring his blood line's continuation by several more copulations. Then the impregnated doe and the fathering buck go their separate, disinterested ways, not meeting again except by chance encounter.

Back to the point in the reproduction story-line where the buck finds the doe's message in the scrape. If our hunter happened on the scrape before the buck's return and went through the antics described, the story ends there.

The buck will usually abandon a contaminated scrape entirely, despite the doe's urgent message. As important as reproduction is, his own self-preservation comes first. He must stay alive if he is to pass on his genes to another generation. He may work the other scrapes on his line, but chances are he will abandon the entire area altogether, and start over again with a new scrape line somewhere else. If the buck is spooked enough, he may go to the next county or township before settling down to his scrape-line routine again.

Treat a rutting scrape like the biggest timber rattler in the world! Stay away from it! Examine it from a long distance with binoculars. If unable to assess the scrape's condition at that distance, climb a tree for a better angle or view. Make sure that the tree climbed is downwind of the scrape, and far away from any approach or exit trails into or from the scrape.

Wear trapper's gloves, the elbow-length or neoprene/rubber kind when scouting, examining scrape areas or entering and leaving the hunting area. Wear rubber boots or rubber-bottomed pacs.

If possible, wear a neoprene rainsuit, too. Leather, cloth, your skin, sweat droplets, even your breath can leave scent deposits that will send the B&C buck snorting. You'll create a dead scrape, with chances only for younger deer, or a good place to hunt on an antlerless day.

If standhunting from a fixed or climbing stand is your forte, select at least four stand sites; again, study the scrape from a distance. Four sites will be necessary to assure having a downwind stand site. The prevailing wind, the opposing wind after frontal passage and the other two transitional wind directions between the prevailing and frontal winds must be reckoned with. If the scrape is unhuntable from all, or any of the four wind directions, select a stand site, or sites, downwind of an approach or exit trail. Just be sure to keep your distance from the trail as you would the scrape.

The last day of the 1991 firearm deer season, I took a 3½-year-old, 8-point whitetail; he weighed 209 pounds. He was working a scrape. The shot was 167 yards with a 7mm-08 Rem. I rejected earlier chances at three smaller scrape inspectors. Examining the downed 8-pointer was the only time I got inside the shot's distance to the scrape.

Treat scrapes like rattlers. Keep your distance. Bide your time for the big guy. It works.

11

Hunting The Second Season

by Richard P. Smith

H unting late-season whitetails with muzzleloader or bow and arrow can be cold and frustrating. Some of the coldest weather of the year commonly occurs during late seasons nationwide. Most times and most places, that makes it difficult to stay comfortable while hunting.

The effects of earlier hunts on deer can add to the challenge of connecting because numerous whitetails have already been removed from the population and those that are left are at their wariest. The surviving bucks are those most adept at avoiding hunters.

However, if you go about it right, late-season hunting can also be the most rewarding. Trophy bucks are taken every year during these hunts and in some cases those animals are the largest whitetails ever tagged by hunters.

That's certainly true for Michigan bowhunter Jerry Pennington who bagged his best buck Dec. 22, 1992. The typical 10-pointer scored 174⅞ qualifying for a place in Boone & Crockett as well as Pope & Young records.

An unusual set of circumstances contributed to Pennington's success on his trophy buck during the state's late bow season. It might work in your favor sometime.

Wet weather that fall prevented farmers from harvesting an estimated 65 percent of corn crops statewide. The area that

Pennington hunts had a lot of standing corn during December and that's where the deer were.

Three rows of an 80-acre cornfield were cut on December 21st and Pennington set up on the ground at the end of a peninsula of tall grass and weeds that extended into the field. The grass and weeds were high enough to conceal him while seated on a stool. It was cold and windy that evening, and Pennington didn't see a deer, but he was sure the biting wind curtailed deer activity. So the next day he was back in the same place.

It didn't take long for whitetails to start appearing in the swath of corn that had been cut. A number of deer were busily feeding when the book buck finally appeared and walked by Jerry's hiding spot no more than 10 yards away.

Standing corn that remains during late season is always a white-tail magnet. Hunting along the edges of those fields as Pennington did is an excellent strategy when deer are bedding in the field.

In situations where whitetails are bedding elsewhere, planning an ambush along their approach trail is best. If deer aren't reaching fields until after legal shooting time, try to set up as close to bedding areas as possible.

Gene Lengsfeld was only about 100 yards from farm fields planted with corn and alfalfa on December 7th when he bagged one of Minnesota's highest scoring typicals. The exceptional 13-pointer that scored 182-4/8 appeared well before dark, at about 3:30 p.m.

Hunters who prefer still-hunting or stalking can sometimes connect by sneaking through standing corn on windy days. Based on Pennington's lack of deer sightings the evening before he got his big buck, still-hunting rather than posting might be the best option when the wind is blowing hard enough to rattle corn stalks. Driving cornfields is another option, especially during muzzleloader seasons. Although standing corn offers super late-season hunting opportunities, the same applies to any quality food supply that's available in your area. All types of agricultural fields with food remaining will attract whitetails during late seasons. So will remaining remnants of fruit and mast crops such as apples, acorns and beechnuts.

Oak trees of one type or another are found over most of North America and whitetails always concentrate where the nuts are abundant. Many Southern states have a variety of oaks and it's not unusual for a number of species to produce nuts at the same time. Acorns from trees that are members of the white oak family are

usually eaten before those from red oaks. Deer often bed in the nearest heavy cover and make daily trips to stands of mast-producing hardwood trees, so plan an ambush along major trails between bedding and feeding areas. Logging operations where hardwood and evergreen trees are being felled can also be late-season hot spots. Whitetails love to browse on these trees. Some of my best late-season hunting has been at or near cuttings. One of my better black powder bucks was ambushed along a major trail leading to a cutting one December. The 11-pointer's rack scored 129⅝. He showed up late in the evening, trailing a pair of antlerless deer.

For morning hunts, select stand sites at or near bedding areas that deer are expected to return to after feeding all night. One December morning I collected a spike buck with a muzzleloader by posting near a bedding area where a bowhunting friend of mine had seen 10- and 6-point bucks a day or two before. When the bigger bucks didn't show up, I took the spike because it was the last day of the season.

Although it's always nice to take a buck with a big rack, any whitetail taken during the late season can be considered a trophy. Late seasons are an excellent time to take antlerless deer, where legal. I've settled for does during many seasons when time was running out and I had not yet seen a buck.

One last late-season tactic that can pay off where it is legal is baiting. Corn, apples and other types of foods that whitetails prefer can help lure them into position for a shot. Although this technique can increase the number of deer late-season hunters are able to see, the method is often overrated in terms of its effectiveness. Antlered bucks frequently shun bait sites until after dark. Baits established on the edge of heavy cover or in cover where whitetails feel comfortable during daylight hours will be most effective during late seasons.

Although most breeding is over by the time late seasons begin, there might still be some does that haven't been bred, especially late-maturing, young does that will be breeding for the first time. If you see any fresh scrapes or rubs, that might be a sign of current breeding activity and hunting nearby could produce action. There is usually lots of competition among bucks that are still alive to breed does that come into heat during late seasons.

The fact that hunting pressure normally drops off during late seasons can work in favor of hunters who take advantage. Whitetails often return to normal activities after hunting pressure declines. It might also be easier to get permission to hunt private property when competition for hunting spots is reduced. Farmers who have been experiencing crop damage from deer are often willing to grant permission to hunt. The same can be true of landowners who have suffered damage to gardens or ornamental plants.

Sure, late-season hunting can be difficult. But it can also provide you with some of the greatest challenges and rewards of the year. I can think of no better Christmas present than a late-December white-tailed buck.

12

Trophy Hunters' Tips

by John E. Phillips

*D*on Taylor came into my taxidermy shop a few years ago on a Friday afternoon with a tremendous 8-point buck. It was one of the biggest whitetails to come in all season. I commented to Don that this buck would be the trophy of a lifetime for most hunters.

But when I questioned him about how and where he had taken the deer, Don said, "Oh, this buck isn't really the buck I was hunting. I was hunting one bigger than this. I expect to take him over the weekend, and I should have him here for you to mount on Monday."

I laughed at the bravado of this veteran hunter, although Taylor had proven himself on earlier hunts together with me. I could believe that Babe Ruth could stand at the plate with two strikes, point over the center field fence indicating he would hit a home run on the next pitch and then make good on the promise. But, as you can imagine, I was skeptical when a hunter told me that within two days he would bag a trophy buck—unless he was going to buy the deer at a game ranch.

I ended up eating those thoughts. Bright and early the following Monday morning, Taylor hauled in the trophy buck he had promised. It was indeed bigger than the deer he had brought me on Friday!

With a confident grin, Don explained that he had been hunting this buck for three years. "During that time, I learned where this buck moved in daylight hours and the routes he took to and from bedding areas. I had found what he did when hunting pressure built up. I identified the open spots he had to cross throughout the day. Since this weekend was the first one of the rifle season, I knew he would bury in thick cover as soon as he felt the increase of hunting pressure. I just went to the spot where I had decided the buck must be. Then when he showed up, I took him."

As a writer, I have come to see the common denominator among all great writers is they study how other great writers write and read the writings of great writers. This same type of learning process should also be able to help me learn how to hunt big bucks. So, over the years I have studied the people who consistently bring big deer into my taxidermy shop year after year. Here's some of the traits most of these men have had.

They Get To Know The Deer

Most of us go deer hunting to take a buck—any buck—but preferably a large buck. However, the trophy hunter is hunting only one buck. He learns all he can about that deer and is not interested in squeezing the trigger on any buck except the particular animal he is hunting.

"I've been hunting the same buck for three years now," Ed McMillan, who has concentrated on hunting trophy bucks most of his life, told me. "This deer has a home range of about eight miles and never beds down in the same place two nights consecutively.

"Several property owners tell me when they spot this deer. As of yet, this buck doesn't have a consistent pattern of where he will show up when. Each year I gather more and more information about this monster-sized buck. If old age doesn't claim him, I eventually should be able to find a place in the woods to take him."

To be a trophy hunter like McMillan, you must locate a particular piece of land with a trophy buck on it. Not all lands hold big bucks.

If no trophy buck is on the property you hunt, then you have to find the land where a trophy buck lives, obtain permission to hunt that property, and then probably spend all your hunting time for the next two or three years learning the haunts and habits of that buck. At the same time, you must stay far enough away from the animal not to drive him out of the region.

Consistently successful hunters get to know the individual deer in a specific hunting area as well, or better, than they know their neighbors on their street.

They Use Different Tactics

If you want to bag a trophy buck, don't utilize the same hunting strategies everyone else in the area uses. Deer pattern people just as people pattern deer. Older age class bucks know what most of the hunters do each season and where they go.

One hunter who brought three nice bucks into my taxidermy shop over a 4-year period explained, "I always enter the woods before daylight and come out after dark, whether I take a deer or not. I always go in by water wearing waders or in a boat and leave by water. Then there is no evidence I ever have been in the woods. I leave no scent, candy wrappers or any other telltale signs of where I am hunting. When I take a stand, I am no more than 5 to 10 yards away from the water I've used to get to my stand. By leaving no sign in the woods for other hunters to see or deer to smell, I drastically increase my odds for taking the bigger and better bucks."

Dr. Robert Sheppard, a sportsman who often puts in more than 100 days per season hunting deer makes a unique observation. Sheppard believes that any time you leave a marker on a tree where you put your tree stand or any other type of marker in the woods which other hunters can see and identify, you reduce the chances of that site being a place where you can bag an older age class buck. "If a novice hunter finds a stand site, he'll hunt in that area because he doesn't know where else to hunt," Dr. Sheppard said. "Often he will hunt with the wind blowing from his back, which means his human odor will spook the deer you are trying to take. If you don't prevent other hunters from finding your spots, these places will quickly become unproductive."

Don Taylor hunts in the thickest cover he can locate because he knows that is where trophy bucks must stay to survive hunting season.

"Even in extremely dense cover, there will be some kind of creek, drainage ditch or small open area where you may only be able to see 10 to 15 yards," Taylor reported. "If you go into these areas and hunt these small openings or drainages through thick cover, you will find the larger deer. Even if I spook a deer, I don't really get upset, since in most instances the deer does not know what has spooked him. I've learned if I remain in that same spot, often the buck will return to investigate. When he does, I can take him."

Some hunters seem to have the knack of bagging older age class bucks regularly while hunting public lands where hunting pressure is very high. The unique insight they seem to share is they realize on state game lands the hunters and the deer are constantly on the move from daylight to dark.

One trophy hunter said, "I have found the only place the deer and the hunters are not constantly moving is in very thick cover where visibility is only 10 to 20 yards. I pinpoint these thick cover areas on public game lands before the season. I wait until the end of the season to hunt these spots, however, because I want hunting pressure to force the big bucks to be in these thick cover regions. On the last week of the season, I go into these thickets long before daylight. I want to be on my stand and sitting still at least 45 minutes to an hour before day begins to break.

"I'll remain on that stand until I take a buck or until I can't see my hand in front of my face because of darkness. I eat on my stand, and if I have to go to the bathroom, I carry equipment to take care of that problem, too. Since I am the only thing not moving in the woods during that weekend, I regularly take older and bigger bucks than the other hunters do."

They Have The Personalities Of Trophy Deer Hunters

Most of the true trophy hunters I know are reclusive people. You won't find them in a large group of outdoorsmen telling others about the tactics they have used or the big bucks they have taken. Their hunts are as private and as personal as the courtships of their spouses. A trophy hunter realizes if he tells where and how he is hunting, he gives out the information that will allow others to take the deer he is trying to bag.

Often years of in-the-field experience are required to learn how to consistently take a trophy whitetail. During that time, the sportsman may not harvest another animal. The true trophy hunter bags few deer and tells few people how he finds and takes the animals he does harvest.

I've known some sportsmen who have hunted for 125 consecutive days in one deer season to try and find and take trophy bucks with bow and arrow, black-powder rifle or conventional firearms, yet never bag an animal. When I meet that sort of hunter, I know he's the kind of person likely to be hauling a huge buck into my shop someday. That's because rather than being discouraged, the next year these hunters will log the same number of hours in pursuit of those older age class bucks.

A trophy deer hunter is a relentless scouter. The week after deer season, he will be in the woods attempting to locate the trophy buck that has eluded him all year. When the deer begin to drop their

Years of pursuit pay off when you finally get that trophy deer in your sights. If you settle for a lesser deer, you can't kill a trophy.

antlers, he will be in the forest finding the sheds of the big bucks no one else has taken. As the bucks begin to grow their antlers in the summer, he will go into the woods and crop lands to scout and learn the habits and hideouts of the trophy buck he will hunt the next season.

A trophy hunter will begin to hunt without a bow or gun the deer he plans to take at least a month before the season opens. He will know when that deer changes food sources. He will locate the animal's bed and the routes the buck has traveled to and from the bed. He will have as much information on that one trophy buck as a football coach will have on the opposing team.

The difference between the trophy hunter and most hunters is the trophy hunter is willing to pay the high price of time, energy and hard work to be the best in his sport. The consistently successful trophy buck hunter:

* has learned patience and perseverance.

*is willing to spend hundreds of hours each season researching the animal he hunts.

*is confident about his ability to bag older age class bucks.

*will end the season not bagging a buck if he does not have the opportunity to take the animal he has been hunting all season.

*does not try to impress others with his trophies or his hunting knowledge.

The contest is between the deer and the trophy hunter. No spectator or applause is sought or required.

The true trophy hunter is the consummate student. When he finally bags that buck of a lifetime, he immediately starts to research another trophy deer to hunt.

However, a price must be paid for excellence in any sport. Most of us just "get lucky" when we take big deer. But a few, rare individuals dedicate themselves to becoming the best deer hunters they can be. These are the ones who have earned the right to be called trophy whitetail hunters.

Locating
Trophy Bucks

1

20 Tips For Close-To-Home Trophy Bucks

by Jeff Murray

For most hunters, talk of a trip to Alberta for a trophy whitetail, or an extra season across the border in Mexico remains just that—talk. The reason is, of course, that most of us are on strictly budgeted time schedules. The gap between talking about an extended hunt and doing it is a wider canyon than Washington can throw a coin across.

And those few who do manage to pull off such a trip more often than not return with a severe case of the wait-until-next-year blues. Having big bucks around you is one thing. Killing one is another matter. It seems that just when a hunter gets to know an area well enough to move in for the kill, it's time to go home.

Big bucks are different, and it takes time to figure them out. That's why average hunters using average tactics will generally score average deer.

Just suppose time wasn't a problem. And suppose you've got bucks with decent racks close by. What would your odds be of scoring on that buck of a lifetime? Very good, to say the least.

One of the big stories in the world of white-tailed deer hunting has been all the trophies that are being taken within commuting distance of "lucky" hunters. It could happen to you, regardless of where you live, because deer populations are at all-time highs.

Hunting close to home, however, takes as much skill as an out-of-town adventure. In fact, it takes more planning, and more grit to be successful at it. I've seen scores of good hunters blow it.

What follows is a rundown of some areas I know that harbor bucks. Apply the generalities to your locale, and see if you don't agree.

Special Hunts

Each fall, special lottery-type hunts are organized for public lands to keep the deer numbers in check. At the top of the list are state parks and state and national wildlife refuges. Some support a limited hunting season every year, while others are open only when the park manager, or district offices, deem it appropriate.

The key is to be on top of the situation and not let one slip by unnoticed. A good way to avoid this is to cultivate a relationship with field personnel in order to stay on top of game trends.

Also, collect game regulations (the booklets you receive when you buy a hunting license). They list these "extra" hunts along with deadlines and addresses for applications.

Check Out Suburbia

The reason deer thrive in the suburbs is because of the habitat. There are plenty of places to eat and hide. Your challenge is to discern the two, and plot a strategy that's best suited to the terrain, time of the year and weather conditions.

A shortcut to this process is the little-known soil conservation map. These maps indicate soil types, drainage patterns and watersheds. This is where most of the deer will be, and by overlaying an aerial photograph with a good soil map, logical hot spots will emerge.

Consider Golf Courses

The local golf course is a great place for a buck to hang around. Witness Bill Kontras' No. 2 Pope & Young monster. It was a links junkie because the early green shoots in the spring, the cover and the abundant source of water made life easy.

Surprisingly, greens keepers hate deer and might accommodate your plea to hunt their lands. Deer, you see, ruin plush fairways and greens with their sharp hooves, and eat sprouting vegetation. It's possible to get permission to hunt a golf course, but it won't be easy (safety and liability are the main concerns). Don't fret. Ask adjoining property owners.

Scour River Bottoms

Most deer stay where they ought to, and a lush river bottom will always be at the top of their list, when available. Food doubles as security cover, so what more could a whitetail want?

Problem is, most hunters know this, and competition can be tough. Select an access point that's slightly out of the way.

Hunt From A Fence Line

Top bowhunter Myles Keller uses too obvious but always overlooked fence lines to great advantage. There's a reason nobody has taken more Pope & Young trophies than Keller, and fence lines are an integral part of his strategy.

"From a fence line I can 'prehunt' while I'm scouting," he says. "I have a full 360-degree field of view, and the bonus of a buck every so often is hard to beat."

Keller chooses fence lines judiciously. He prefers those that string out from woodlots, but also bisect row crops. Deer are more likely to use them than those that have no nearby cover.

Hunt Food Plots

Minnesota's best whitetail came from a 20-acre cornfield. And why not? The deer was undisturbed for three years. The corn provided an ideal daytime bedding lair.

But hunting corn is hardly a panacea. Where do you put up a stand? How do you see? Smart hunters have learned to look for sign on tree lines bordering such food plots, then erect a stand that's strategically located to cover the tree line and cornfield.

Discover A Swamp Island

Swamps, like lakes, look pretty uniform on the surface. But with a critical eye, it's amazing what irregularities you'll find. A swamp island is the perfect counterpart to a reef in a lake.

Swamp islands can be found with topo maps. First, locate swamps with the marsh symbol. Then look for small circles or doughnut-shaped double-circles within the marsh. The lines on a topo map connect points of equal elevation, and the circles tell you where there's a little knoll.

What makes swamp islands so attractive to bucks is an obvious reprieve from hunter pressure; few hunters know about them, and even fewer hunt them. But forget about hunting them if the wind isn't perfect. The deer will scent you and likely abandon the island.

Don't Drive By Highway Corridors

One Halloween night I almost hit the biggest deer I'd ever seen. It was standing broadside in the middle of an interstate highway when my lights reflected off its eyes. Undaunted, it ambled into the woods. After I carefully marked the spot, I returned the following week, to find a stretch of land laced with deer sign.

For some reason, hunters think that deer live only off of dirt roads. Not so. If you take the time to scout lands along freeways and four-laners, you'll find plenty of deer and very few hunters.

Find Private Woodlots Adjacent To Public Lands

If I could pick one landowner to befriend, this is the one I'd choose. Deer don't care if land is public or private, but they do know where the fewest hunters are.

Better yet, knock on the door of privately-owned tracts within a heavily-hunted wildlife management unit. If food plots are close by, all the better. But when you ask, look civil. Don't come in camo clothing. Wear a dress shirt and maybe a tie. I like to bring my 10-year-old son along on occasion. These folks need to know that hunters are real people with real jobs and real families—just like them.

Hunt WMAs On The Pheasant Opener

I still remember it like it was yesterday. It was 1981, opening day of pheasant season. Glowing predictions for a great bird season sent shotgunners marching abreast through shoulder-high cover. I was one of them.

But when I reached the end of a shelterbelt that formed a neat "T" with a ditchbank, I wasn't thinking of roosters. A bowhunter was about to put a knife to the belly of a dandy 10-point buck. We had pushed the deer to the hunter, and it was no accident.

"Happens almost every year," he confessed reluctantly. "You have to be quick, though."

Make Efficiency Your Main Ally

To do this, set up a milk run of hotspots that can be hit one by one. That way, you'll avoid hop-scotching all over the countryside, dictated by last-moment whims and fancies.

Plot Each Area On A Map

This will give you the big picture, as well as the most logical travel routes. The perfect map for this is a township fire map. It isn't too cluttered with detail, like the individual maps you might want to construct for each spot, but it has enough information to keep you on track. If fire maps aren't available, use county highway maps.

Invest In Good Binoculars

They aren't just for Western hunts. When I obtained a pair of Steiner 15X80s, I soon discovered that a lengthy, tedious scouting ordeal can be less painful and more effective. The price is worth it when you consider that you can watch deer totally undetected, without them knowing you're on the same planet.

By "high-power" I'm referring to optics with a magnification between 15 and 20. You will need a tripod, however, but today's light-weight aluminum models fold down to a compact 3- by 14-inch rectangle. The window of your vehicle, rolled up a bit, will also provide stability.

Visit Areas Regularly

By checking every spot personally, you'll be able to keep tabs on sudden shifts in deer movements. You know that there's no substitute for being in the right place a the right time, and this is the best way to do it.

Use A Buddy System

Obviously, a little help from one of your friends can go a long way toward accomplishing the above goals. Two guys can split up the chores of field work, after dividing the hunting territory into zones.

For example, if your partner lives closer to several key spots, let him monitor them. And when an area or two gets hot, you can double up.

Consider Baiting

Nothing can tell you as much about a new area as fast as a

prudent ration of cracked corn. If you fail to generate a lot of white-tail activity within a couple of days, move on. But be sure to check state regulations before baiting.

Ask The Right People

The milk man, propane gas man and UPS driver can save you a lot of time. They travel rural areas on a regular basis, covering their beat as thoroughly as anyone. If a deer with a decent rack dwells in a certain area, chances are one of these individuals will see it.

Hunt The Rut Hard

Every fall I watch hunters burn themselves out prematurely. Just when it's time to deliver a knock-out punch, they don't have anything to give. They sleep in and have a hard time concentrating. There is no antidote, just preventive medicine: Avoid spreading yourself too thin, get needed rest, and be ready for action.

Carry Your Hunting Gear With You

I stash mine in two doubled-sealed plastic trash bags. They're in the back of the pickup whether I'm going to church or to the store. You never know when a buck might appear in the open for a close shot. It happens, and you need to be ready.

Hunt The Same Spots Over The Years

Eventually, patterns will emerge. For reasons only God knows, deer exhibit certain behavior in certain locales. Only experience will show you what it is.

And when you invest time in your own backyard, you won't have to listen to, "You should have been here last week."

2

Hunting High-Country Whitetails

by John Haviland

*L*ast summer my family and I started up a trail into the Bitterroot Mountains. The footpath left the road in a gentle climb, but within a mile it turned straight up the mountain.

As we neared timberline, the flash of running game startled us.

"Deer!" yelled my son, Brian.

At more than 8,000 feet of elevation, I was sure these would be mule deer. The four animals finally stepped into the open. Whitetails! Then they ran down the mountain.

I knew whitetails had been expanding in population and range across the Rocky Mountains, but this was ridiculous. These river bottom and foothills deer were knocking on the door of the Rocky Mountain goat.

After that experience, I read wildlife studies and talked to wildlife biologists, to find out why white-tailed deer have moved up from their traditional river bottoms to the mountains of the Western United States and Canada.

Explorers Lewis and Clark, on their trip across the Bitterroot Mountains, noticed large burns in the Lochsa River region of northern Idaho. Some of these fires were set by Indians along the trails to destroy the forest and encourage grass to grow for their horses. Without Smokey Bear to snuff them out, these fires made large openings in the forest, producing summer and winter range for mule deer and elk.

Fighting forest fires in the early years of this century was still a losing battle. A wet burlap sack, a shovel and a whipsaw made a poor defense against a fire running up a mountain. Fires into the 1930s cleared thousands of square miles of forests while early day foresters looked on. A fire in northern Idaho in 1931 burned thousands of acres of river bottom that had been whitetail range. Whitetails almost disappeared from the area while mule deer moved in to feed on the new brushy fields. Not until many years later, when the brush gave way to a cover of mixed-age conifers, were the whitetails able to take over again.

The forest received a break with the coming of heavy equipment, airplanes and trained fire fighters. The burned-over mountain sides grew up in conifer forests. Forest fires were suppressed at every opportunity.

Bob Henderson is the wildlife biologist with the Montana Fish, Wildlife and Parks for the northern Bitterroots of Montana. Henderson said the higher elevations of the mountains have a much denser cover now than before the 1930s. "Back then the mountain sides were pretty much wide open or had open stands of big ponderosa pines," Henderson said. "Now they're filled in with stands of Douglas fir." The white-tailed deer that used to remain checked in the river bottoms have found a new home in the mountains.

More than a decade of mild winters in the northern Rockies has also helped whitetails expand. The mild weather has allowed more young deer to survive. Without the stress of winter, a doe may produce twins. During tough winters, a doe may conceive every fall, but only produce a fawn every other spring.

An indication of this growth is the increased number of whitetails taken through the game check station near Darby on the southern end of Montana's Bitterroots. In the 1960s, fewer than a dozen whitetails a year were checked through the stop. In the 1980s, the numbers started to increase, and during the 1991 season hunters brought through 179 whitetails.

In 1988, for the first time in Region Two—which covers the Bitterroot, Clark Fork and Blackfoot River drainages—more whitetails than mule deer were harvested. Hunters reported seeing whitetails up to 7,000 and 8,000 feet of elevation in the Bitterroot Mountains.

Roger Hankel, a taxidermist in Missoula, Montana, said in recent years hunters have discovered the expanding whitetail herds. Hankel receives a dozen whitetail bucks to mount for every mule deer buck.

A popular idea for magazine articles has been how mule deer in recent years have started behaving like whitetails. I have found the reverse with these mountain whitetails. They share some of the same characteristics as mule deer.

Mule deer now have to share mountain habitat with expanding whitetail populations.

When a mule deer jumps up and runs off, the old advice said to wait a minute before shooting because the buck would stop for one last look before it ran out of sight. Mule deer did this not because they were dumb, but to pinpoint the exact location of danger before expending all the energy to flee up a steep mountain face.

On the final day of deer season a couple falls ago, I tagged along with a friend of mine and his wife. Corey had saved his tag all season looking for Mr. Big Buck and was prepared to eat his tag if the right buck failed to appear. His wife, B.J., on the other hand, had spent every weekend of the season studying for her accounting classes at the local university. B.J. was ready for a good hike and a chance at some deer steaks.

We drove to the mountains at the edge of town and started hiking in a drizzle. A doe flushed in front of us in the dark. She stopped above, stamped her fore leg and snorted. We kept climbing, and by the time shooting light had dawned we were high up the mountain.

A white-tailed buck jumped from the edge of an opening in the forest. The buck ran up the side of a finger ridge with its tail clamped down. He stopped short of the crest and looked back. The white hair around the buck's tail stood erect, signaling the deer was ready to flee. B.J. brought her rifle up as she sat on the ground. Unfortunately, the lens caps were still on the scope. She tore at the rubber band holding on the caps, but the buck had seen enough. Its tail came up as it skipped the last steps to the ridge top and ran down the far side.

We jumped two more bucks that morning, and later that afternoon everything fell into place. B.J. spotted a deer running off a steep ridge. The deer stopped to look around and when it did, B.J. was ready with her .30-06 resting on her knees.

Concern has been raised about whitetails competing with mule deer on the same range and possibly pushing the mule deer out. Henderson believes the only serious competition between the two deer may develop when they are crowded onto the same lowland winter ranges.

Higher in the mountains, during the summer and fall, the two deer have different food preferences. Mule deer tend to eat more grasses and drier browse than whitetails. Whitetails have smaller teeth than mule deer and are much more selective of what they eat, leaning toward succulent plants that are easy to nip off and chew.

Because of the whitetails' preference for moist foods, the best place to look for them in the mountains is near springs and along creeks. The best spots for whitetails are also the best for mountain grouse.

A couple Septembers ago, I was hunting grouse in the mountains. I hiked across the dry hillsides, going from one spring to the next. At each spring I made a weaving circle to look for grouse. Sometimes I jumped blue grouse, other times ruffed grouse and often as not no grouse.

A covey of blue grouse roosted above a green patch of clover growing over a seep in the timber. They waddled to the edge of a steep ridge when they saw me, flying one at a time off the ridge. My first two shots missed, but on the third I remembered to pull ahead and below the diving bird. The grouse hit the ground.

As the grouse was still tumbling, a glint of antlers caught the edge of my view. I knew it was a buck and immediately wished I had my bow instead of my shotgun. The buck cleared the deadfall where it had been hiding and ran across a glimpse of an opening. I half expected a mule deer, but wasn't disappointed when the deer was a big whitetail. The buck stopped for a moment at the same drop off as the grouse. With a flick of its tail the buck pitched off the edge and was gone.

Although that buck was hiding under the dense cover of the forest, he wasn't making his living there. The closed canopy of an old forest blocks most of the sunlight from reaching the ground and creates a barren understory. These mountain whitetails need a broken canopy of conifers for hiding cover that lets in enough sunlight to grow stands of browse like red osier dogwood, western red cedar, redstem ceanothus and serviceberry. These favorite plants far from cover, though, will go untouched. Remember, whitetails prefer good cover over good food.

With the first snows of winter, and often with as little change as the first frosts, whitetails descend to easier living. Depending on the country, the deer might drop elevation down to a foothill slope with a good exposure to the sun, or travel 10 or more miles to a river bottom to yard up for the winter.

There is a mountain at about 6,500 feet of elevation that I hunt from September to December. All summer and into early fall, the whitetails hang out along the creeks leading up the mountain and in the moist quaking-aspen groves. A couple friends and I made a drive there once while bowhunting. I hid along a narrow creek, figuring the spooked deer would remain in the cover as they fled. I barely had enough time to place an arrow on the string of my bow when the sound of snapping twigs came from up the creek. The noise came closer and then was there, as a buck shot past me.

The buck ran by so fast I had to freeze. The only good look I got at his antlers showed a five by five rack.

By the middle of November these whitetails have moved to the lower sagebrush foothills. They stick to the taller sage and thickets of young ponderosa pines. The best way I've found to hunt them is to sit on a vantage point early and late in the day when the deer come to the edges to feed.

One frosty morning I glassed these foothills, carefully looking into the edges of the woods. Not spotting anything, I decided to move. As I was strolling through the sage I had just glassed, a buck jumped up and stood looking. The buck glanced up and down the mountain trying to decide which way to run. My rifle came up and didn't give him the choice. The sun had just started to shine over the mountain as I walked toward the white of the buck's tail that marked where it had fallen deep in the cover.

3

City's Edge Whitetails

by Glenn Sapir

As you head north along the Great White Way, theater marquees trimmed with hundreds of lights brighten the crowded sidewalks that line Broadway. Uptown the theaters give way to chic boutiques and upscale restaurants and bars. The crowds are thinner, but present nonetheless. Eventually, you leave Manhattan and enter the Bronx, where the apartment buildings stand taller. Not far from Broadway, to the east, is Yankee Stadium, perhaps the biggest single parcel of grass in the immediate area.

If you head even farther north, you'll eventually leave New York City, but it will be hard to tell from the landscape. Buildings, maybe not as tall or as numerous, still reach to the sky, and gray asphalt still lines the sidewalks. Were it not for the infield of Yonkers Raceway or some county parks, large patches of green would be seldom seen.

When you left the Bronx, you indescernibly entered Westchester County. It is an area that is contained by the Hudson River to its west, the Long Island Sound to the east. Its northern border is suburban/semi-rural Putnam County, and to its northeast, the affluent suburb of Fairfield County, Connecticut.

In the county's 450 square miles are cities, towns and villages. Some of New York State's poorest citizens live in rundown tenements here; some of the nation's wealthiest dwell on several-acre estates. Rich or poor, nearly a million people call Westchester County home.

This setting doesn't sound like a hunter's paradise. However, Westchester County has consistently produced outstanding trophy white-tailed bucks to the bow—the only legal big game hunting tool here. It also has been the laboratory for an experimental deer management program that many sportsmen, game managers, and landowners are applauding.

"With the way human populations are growing across the nation," observes Mike Chirico, "I think more and more areas are going to adopt the program we have initiated in Westchester."

Actually, game managers on Long Island and in western New York have already adopted Westchester's plan, and other states have made inquiries.

Chirico, a railroad employee and partner in Buchanan Sports, a popular retail shop for hunters in Westchester, has played an active role in shaping deer hunting regulations in his home county.

He was one of the founders of the Westchester Bowhunters Association in 1978 and served as the organization's first president.

Let Chirico start tracing for you how the regulations developed.

"We formed the Westchester Bowhunters Association in 1978 to protect and improve our sport in Westchester County. In a year we had 250 members!

"By working hand-in-hand with the New York State Department of Environmental Conservation (DEC)—Glenn Cole, wildlife manager; Steve Cook, conservation officer; and Dick Henry, biologist—and with landowners, we have been able to accomplish a lot," Chirico says.

"First of all, back when I was a child, the bowhunting season was two months long. Then, because of hound hunters or bird hunters who thought the bowhunters' presence in the woods was a problem, they cut us back to one month—November 1 to December 1.

"When the Westchester Bowhunters Association was formed, we decided that was the first thing we needed to tackle. We put in a resolution, and we got back our two-month season [November 1-December 31]," he continued.

With access limited by virtually no public land in the county on which to legally bowhunt deer, even a two-month season did little to stem the growth of the deer herd.

Following the greenbelts along north-south highways, deer began showing up in southern municipalities as well as all across the greener, less populated, northern half of the county. Car-deer collisions became common. Expensive ornamental plantings around homes, as well as trees and crops on the few remaining orchards and truck farms in Westchester, became favored targets for browsing whitetails.

Another nemesis came on the scene—the black-legged, or deer tick—and Westchester County soon became the nation's epicenter of the Lyme Disease outbreak. White-tailed deer were reputed to be a key carrier of the tick. Even in a county that was a hotbed of anti-hunting propaganda, the realities of a deer population out of balance with its environment became evident.

"In the mid-'80s, the association petitioned through the Westchester Conservation Council that the county be granted the same privilege that Deer Management Units (DMU's) across the state were given," recalls Chirico.

The DMU system in other parts of New York enabled licensed hunters to apply for permits for particular areas that would allow them to take deer of either sex, in addition to the deer they were permitted to take under their statewide big game license. Westchester, through the bowhunters' efforts and the support of regional deer managers, was given that same privilege, which now is two additional DMU permits.

"Then, along came Dick Henry," says Chirico, speaking of the biologist as if he were some kind of savior.

Henry is a full-time deer biologist for Region 3, the regional office of the DEC that supervises management in Westchester County.

"Westchester had been identified as a deer management problem area because, first, the only legal means of hunting was archery, and second, hunting access was very limited," Henry says.

"The Westchester County Executive had appointed a Blue Ribbon Committee—a mixed bag of the population, including landowners, hunters, business people, and others to make recommendations on the deer population," the biologist says, "and the committee recommended a reduction of the deer herd."

The low harvest had allowed deer to grow old. That's why so many big bucks inhabited Westchester.

"The first year we allowed multiple [two] DMU permits, hunters could take deer of either sex," Henry says. "The plan didn't work."

Why?

"Because the hunters only went after bucks," Henry says.

Then in 1992, the deer management plan was refined, introducing the concept that has been opening eyes across the country.

"We set aside a specific number of bonus tags," Henry says, "for hunters who bagged an antlerless deer."

During the 1992 season a hunter, for each antlerless deer he tagged with a DMU permit, could receive a bonus tag, good for either a buck or doe. If he bagged an antlerless deer on that tag, he could come back in for yet another bonus tag, and so on, until the tags ran out.

"The idea came to me in a tree stand," Henry says, but the results would suggest he certainly had his feet on the ground when he fine-tuned the strategy.

That first year, Westchester bowhunters doubled the previous year's deer take—and quadrupled the doe harvest. When the Westchester Bowhunters Association was formed, the deer take in Westchester was about 200, according to Chirico. In 1992, the harvest climbed to more than 2,000!

For appearance more than management, the DEC refined the program in 1993 limiting each hunter to two bonus tags. Still, coupled with Westchester being included in 1992 in the statewide regulation that allows a successful bowhunter to get another general-season tag if successful with the bow, recreational opportunities have increased considerably. In fact, last year a Westchester bowhunter could take as many as four antlered bucks and two antlerless deer!

At the same time, the DEC has maximized the herd management potential of a bow-only hunting season.

"We still have too many deer," Henry says. "Hunters have to target more adult does."

In fact, at a meeting of the Westchester County Bowhunters Association, Henry illustrated the problem.

"Bucks in Westchester are servicing does as late as April," he said. "The does are going into estrus over and over again so that they will be bred. We've undertaken a study of road-killed does in the spring to evaluate when the fetuses they are carrying were conceived. The deer that are conceived later are less likely to survive the stresses of the next winter."

A 6-point buck, with his antlers intact, was spotted dead along the Taconic State Parkway in a central Westchester location—on March 24!

"Sure," Henry says, "their testosterone level is still up then; they're still participating in breeding activities."

The Westchester Bowhunters Association has helped do more than simply refine regulations. When the state began to compile a list of landowners who complained of deer damage, members found a place to hunt, and landowners were pleased with the quiet solution to their problems. Later, when Lyme Disease began its spread through Westchester County, other landowners sought the help of association members.

When the Westchester Medical Center needed volunteers for its promising Lyme Disease vaccine study, its leaders appealed to the Westchester Bowhunters Association.

"I spoke to the group at one of its meetings, and several volunteers signed up," says Donna McKenna, nurse practitioner and assistant to the vaccine-development program's leader.

Each year bowhunters bring to an association meeting their trophy racks for official scoring and entry in their big deer contest. Big bucks come out of Westchester every year, and the fact that recreational hunting is increasing in the county is a tribute to active sportsmen, receptive game managers, and understanding landowners who make their property available to sportsmen.

Mike Chirico might be right. You might see similar regulations adopted in your state!

4

Blue-Collar Book Bucks

by Glenn Sapir

When a hunter etches his name in the record books six times in six years, you might draw certain conclusions. You might imagine a free-spender devoting significant resources to hiring the best professional guides and outfitters in renowned destinations, such as Saskatchewan and Texas. You probably picture a tense, call it "obsessive," determination to become immortalized in hunting archives. Quite likely you'd conjure up an image of a young athlete, physically equipped to meet the rigors that the special stresses presented in hunting exclusively for big bucks.

Enter Mike Chirico, 53-year-old engineer for Metro North, a New York commuter railroad, and a member of the North American Hunting Club. Since 1989, Chirico has bagged several bucks with his bow, shotgun and muzzleloader, including a half-dozen that have received record-book recognition. Four of them have been included in the New York State Big Bucks Club record book; four have garnered archery's Pope and Young Club recognition; and one earned a place in both the Boone and Crockett Club and the National Muzzle Loading Association's Long Hunter Society archives.

Chirico hasn't traveled across the continent to buy the best opportunities for trophy bucks. In fact, four of his six giants have been taken within a half-hour of his home, Buchanan, New York—a suburb on the Hudson River some 40 miles north of the Big Apple. The other two, including the Boone and Crockett and Long

Hunter Society monster, were shot on a Maryland farm on the Eastern Shore.

At age 53, Chirico could hardly be called a young athlete. Though physically fit, he still says, "I like to hunt with my son—not only for his company, but to help drag out the deer."

Though Chirico is an avid deer hunter, calling him "obsessed" would be unfair. Instead, you could describe Mike Chirico as a dedicated deer hunter, intent on harvesting big bucks. He works for his deer, before the season in preparation and during the season with hunting know-how. Chirico hasn't come up with any truly revolutionary techniques. He's simply a blue-collar hunter whose hard-work ethic pays off. I guess you could call him an Everyman's role model, and no doubt you could learn something from him.

Ask him to what he attributes his success, and he'll tell you in his typical modest demeanor:

"Thirty-nine years of mistakes."

After the chuckling subsides, in a more serious moment, he'll tell you it's "being in the right place at the right time." How does he maximize the chance of "being in the right place at the right time?"

"Practicing is the key," says Chirico. There is no "right time," if you aren't prepared to make the shot when it presents itself.

Because bowhunting is the only legal form of deer hunting in Westchester, his home county, that is the sport to which he devotes most of his attention. He practices religiously at a 3-D range, and has set up a target in his backyard.

"Whenever I can fit it in, I am practicing," the hunter says. "There's nothing more important to success! You have to know when to release your arrow on the different shots, such as quartering away and broadside."

Another important preseason activity is locating land and securing permission to hunt. In Westchester County, not an acre of public land is open to hunting. So Chirico must look to private landowners as his key to access. In affluent, suburban northern Westchester County, huntable tracts are usually estates of five acres or more.

"I'll drive the roads, keeping my eyes open," Chirico says. "I'll look for yards that have deer fences. In the winter I'll search for landscaping that is protected by burlap. I'll keep my eyes open for an evident browse line on someone's trees."

Not only does he keep his eyes open. His ears are permanently attuned to opportunities.

"I am always listening, whether I am waiting in line at a delicatessen or mingling at a house party. When a guy says, 'The deer are eating me out of house and home,' I'm ready to come to his rescue."

But there's more to it than that:

"In suburban areas, you must get a landowner's trust and respect. My keys are a handshake, an introduction and credentials. I like to emphasize that I have been a New York State bowhunter education instructor since the program's inception and a North American Hunting Club member. That often seems to mean a lot."

The right contacts can include people other than landowners. Chirico, for example, has long been an active member of the Westchester County Bowhunters Association. "By going to meetings and making friends, I've come to learn about hunting opportunities in the area that I wouldn't have otherwise," he says.

Of course, scouting the land to which he has access is another essential part of Chirico's hunting preparation. "I've taken 10 white-tailed bucks from the same tree on a four-acre parcel. I know where the bucks travel in that woodlot." What does he look for when scouting?

"There are three main ways I can identify whether an area is holding a big buck," Chirico explains. "Everyone knows to look for scrapes. Well, I look for big scrapes. I've seen them the size of a kitchen tabletop or a car hood. When you see one that size, you can bet you are dealing with a very big-bodied deer. You can't be sure that it's wearing a record-book rack, but it's likely a wall-hanger.

"The second sign is rubs. Again, everyone knows rubs are a sign of bucks. But what I'm looking for are rubs not only on saplings, but on bigger trees. When you find a 10-inch-diameter tree that has been rubbed, a trophy is in the woods.

"Third, I put time in just watching. I like to find high spots, take a ground stand before the season, and just watch, becoming, like the animal I am going to hunt, aware of everything around me. That way I'll often make a sighting of the big bucks I will later hunt.

"I'm a firm believer in high spots—small ridges and knolls," he says. "From there deer can wind danger, and see and hear everything. That's where the big bucks are comfortable."

His theory reminds me of Tom Mosher, a remarkably successful deer hunting outfitter in New Brunswick who had long ago espoused to me his belief in "rutting knolls," elevated pieces of land where big bucks in rut would travel. When exploring new hunting areas, Mosher studies topographical maps, looking for elevated ground in swamps and marshes, and if they check out, that is often where he sets up his tree stands.

In Maryland, Chirico's hunting takes place in hardwood lots adjoining soybean and cornfields and marshes on the land that he leases with several other hunters. In either case, tree stands are an essential part of his hunting strategy, and tree stand placement is vital to success.

"I always try to set up so that I am downwind of where I think the big buck is going to be," Chirico says. "I'm also always aware of the background. In Westchester, for instance, the bow season runs from November 1 through all of December. So, for the whole season, the trees are bare, and don't kid yourself: deer look up. If I'm silhouetted against a bare skyline, they'll see me."

Instead, Chirico looks for stands of trees that will conceal his shape, like hemlocks or other evergreens.

"In 1995 I took a 7-pointer with the bow. It wasn't a record-book buck, but it was a nice one. It had seen me in the morning, but that same day I went home for lunch, cut down a branch from a pin oak that still had its dead, brown leaves, and I brought the branch up to my stand. I wired it to the tree behind me—and killed that 7-pointer that afternoon, from the same stand he had spotted me in that morning!"

It's apparent that Chirico not only pays attention to the basics, but is willing to do the little extras necessary to get the big buck. Chirico believes it is important to allow at least a half-hour for the woods to settle down, so he always gets set up early.

"Typically, I will drive to a hunting spot near home and get in the woods a half-hour to 45 minutes before light. I'll pack in my portable tree stand, and I'll pack my one-piece insulated suit in the stand. After the average walk of 1/4 mile to my tree, I'll put on my suit, get my safety belt on, and get set up."

Though many people utilize attractant and cover scents, Chirico's primary precaution is wearing rubber boots.

"I can't tell you how important that is," he says. "I've seen deer come to my trail when I had worn leather boots. They'd scent where I had walked, turn tail and bolt. But when they cross my tracks when I've worn rubber boots, they keep on coming!

"During the season I do use unscented deodorant, and I hang my hunting suit in the garage, away from breakfast, cigarettes and other household odors."

That's the scenario that starts most of Mike's hunts, and it is the one that began a hunt in November 1995. The day before, Mike had collected an 8-pointer with his 60-pound Hoyt bow, so on this morning he told his friend and his son, with whom he was hunting, that he would only take a 9-point or better.

Mike let four young bucks walk, living up to his promise.

"Besides, if you really want to get a big buck, you have to let the smaller ones go by," Chirico insists. "That sounds simple enough, and most hunters know it, but most shoot, anyway, at the first buck that they see!

"In sight of my son, a big buck came over a knoll. It presented me with a shot, and I took it. The buck went 60 yards and died. The arrow had gone through its lungs. It turned out to be a 10-pointer, measuring 140 1/8 and weighing 165 pounds dressed."

Though his lifetime home of Westchester is from where three of his four Pope and Young bucks have come, it was in Maryland that the bruiser that simultaneously got him into the Boone and Crockett Club and Long Hunter Society annals lived and died. It was a special three-day blackpowder hunt falling between bow and gun seasons during late October.

"I made my 1/4-mile hike to a holly tree in a hardwood forest next to a marsh," Chirico says. "In early morning three small bucks came by. I let them go. Then I heard percussion caps misfiring—and almost immediately a stick cracked behind me. I turned to see what looked like a good-size buck some 60 yards away. I aimed my Thompson/Center .50 caliber Renegade and fired. The buck ran 70 yards, out of sight."

Showing the patience of an experienced hunter, Chirico resisted climbing down and following up on the shot immediately.

"I waited three-quarters of an hour, then tracked him," he says. "When I saw him, I couldn't believe his size! The typical 8-point buck later scaled 215 pounds dressed and measured 160⅞ B&C points."

That hunt typified the basics, along with the extras, that Mike Chirico brings to every one of his whitetail hunts. He had scouted the area, situated his tree stand accordingly, and planned his strategy. He let three bucks go by, then relied on the aim much practice had honed.

Maryland is not a renowned deer hunting state, but he was in the right place at the right time, and put his 39 years of learning from his mistakes to work. That day in October Mike Chirico did what any one of us might do if we are willing to follow some of the same rules this fellow NAHC member has carved for himself.

5

Quest For The Southeast's Best Bucks

by Jim Casada

*T*he average whitetail hunter goes through something of an evolution as he becomes more deeply involved in the sport and begins to master its intricacies. When he starts hunting, any deer will do, and even a spike buck is deemed a true trophy. However, he begins to be a bit selective after a few successes.

Recognizing that harvesting does is beneficial to herd management and venison from does is every bit as appealing to the palate as that from yearling bucks, the sportsman adjusts his thinking a bit. He still gets an itchy trigger finger when a 6-pointer appears, but he passes on spikes or forkhorns and harvests more does.

The third phase in this progression usually comes later, after the hunter has taken a respectable 8-pointer or two. This is when big bucks become a fixation. He duly harvests two or three does each year for the family freezer, but most of his hours afield are spent in a tireless quest for old Mossy Horns. He has become a dedicated, maybe even addicted, trophy hunter.

While not all of us might quite reach that stage, I know of no deer hunter who doesn't harbor thoughts of taking a massive, heavy racked deer. Some luck, such as being in the right place at the right time, together with a fair share of skill, is usually involved in shooting such bucks. These considerations aside, though, there is no more important factor in upping your likelihood of claiming a memorable deer than "being there." You need to hunt where there are goodly numbers of quality deer.

In 10 states of the Southeastern United States, from North Carolina south and west to the Mississippi River, certain areas clearly stand out when it comes to quality habitat and the production of large-antlered bucks.

In terms of sheer numbers, Georgia and Kentucky are in a class by themselves. A look at "Records of North American Whitetail Deer," published by the Boone and Crockett Club, clearly tells the story. Appreciably more typical bucks scoring high enough to qualify for listing have been taken in Georgia than in any other Southeastern state, while Kentucky sits atop the list of Southeastern non-typical entries.

At the opposite end of the spectrum, there are few if any for Florida, North Carolina and South Carolina. That should not suggest, however that, you should write off all these states as being unworthy of a trophy quest. Arkansas, Louisiana and Mississippi all have fairly impressive numbers of bucks, upwards of a dozen in each case, qualifying for B&C recognition. Pretty much the same picture holds true in Pope and Young (bowhunting) and Longhunter Society (muzzleloader) record-book listings.

Kentucky offers quite a bit of public hunting land, and I would particularly recommend trying to get drawn for one of the bow or blackpowder hunts held annually on military bases in the state. A couple of years ago I had a misfire on what would have been my "buck of a lifetime" during such a hunt, and that day saw several really impressive deer taken.

In Georgia, three counties—Worth, Dooly, and Macon—have long been heralded as big-buck country. Worth County is particularly recommended with fewer than three typical B&C whitetail coming from within its borders, according to the third edition of "Records of North American Whitetail Deer."

In Arkansas, Desha and Arkansas counties are particularly noteworthy, although it should be mentioned that many record-book Arkansas deer trace back three or four decades. The state's total of 62 entries notwithstanding, it is probably not one of the better places in the Southeast to seek a trophy buck today. Much the same is true of Mississippi, where virtually all the listings date back a decade or more.

On the other hand, Alabama, or at least a portion of it, is richly deserving of a trophy hunter's attention. That state's well-known

Black Belt region, so-called because of its dark, nutrient-rich soil, is producing some truly fine bucks. The Black Belt is home to a number of lodges and commercial hunting operations, many of which have had quality management programs in effect for some time. Add to that the fact that the peak of the rut here comes in January, when hunting is already over for the season in most states, and Alabama becomes a most appealing late-season destination.

Speaking of quality management, hunters might also want to give some thought to South Carolina, along with a portion of the Natchez Trace Wildlife Management Area in Tennessee. South Carolina has an incredible abundance of deer, not to mention the nation's longest season, and some recent initiatives here show great promise. Specifically, this is the state where the Quality Deer Management Association got its start, and the concept has really taken hold in Palmetto Country. Find a club or commercial operation (and there are many of both available) where quality management practices have been in place for several years, and you have a real chance of seeing big bucks. You might even be able to harvest one in velvet in the Low Country, where the season opens on August 15. If possible, try to hunt in a region where lots of soybeans are grown. This protein-rich legume really gives bucks a jumpstart in growth.

On a portion of the Natchez Trace in Tennessee, the Tennessee Wildlife Resources Agency has an ongoing quality management program in place, and this is probably the best public land in the Volunteer State to seek a big buck. Elsewhere, river bottoms and the rich farm lands in the western portion of the state are home to some fine deer.

While record-book bucks are relatively few and far between in the Southeast, years of sensible management, along with a growing emphasis on quality in some areas, means that there are plenty of places in the region where you can take a deer that would impress any hunter. Remember that habitat always plays a key role. Find a fine agricultural region, add good genetics (check on where the deer came from when restocking took place) and look into the availability of places to hunt. You'll have a good start toward finding the buck of your dreams.

6

Scouting: The Key to Post-Rut Success

by Nick Sisley

Wind whipped out of the valley, funneling through the high saddle with bone chilling velocity. High in my tree stand, I scrunched my neck deeper into my hooded parka, at the same time wiggling fingers and toes in hopes of increasing the meager blood circulation that was going on there.

My stand was anything but a comfortable place that morning. The rut had peaked weeks previous. But I was positioned at the low spot along a ridge that ran for several miles. Despite my frozen perch I was alert, for I was overlooking heavily used deer crossings, several of them. Further, this saddle was the easiest place along the ridge for whitetails to cross when pushed from the lower ground on either side of the mountain by rifle-toting redcoats.

Already I had watched three does, each with a pair of fawns, egg-walk their way up from the valley that lay to my northwest. An hour after legal shooting time, an eight-point buck with a 12-inch spread came from the opposite direction—the valley on the other side. As he stood with his head turned almost 180 degrees around, watching his back trail, I placed a 150-grain Remington Bronze Point where it did the most good—the shoulder knuckle on my side.

But, as usual when I'm enthused about divulging some how-to tips, I'm getting ahead of my story. The circumstances surrounding it had started weeks previous, when the bucks in this area were at the height of their rutting behavior, battling shrubs until those stems were now dying ruins. Bucks had pawed the ground and urinated until the stench of this sexual behavior had the immediate areas reeking a musky odor.

The rut is the prime time for scouting, if your state's deer season opens up after the rut, as mine does in Pennsylvania. Traditionally, buck season begins the Monday after Thanksgiving here. The height of the rut tends to take place two to three weeks prior to that. It's when the bucks are the most vulnerable that I'm traipsing behind my pointing dogs, chasing ruffed grouse.

This is also the time that my attention gets focused on rutting whitetail sign, so my interest in ruffs gets sidetracked aplenty. The game plan during the rut should be to put the pieces of the whitetail's lifestyle puzzle together.

Rutting bucks stay on the move. Consequently, they leave more than their normal share of sign relating to their movements. Once the first shot goes off opening morning in a heavily hunted state, the biggest bucks often become solitary, moving as little as possible. However, by discovering how a buck spends his day and night, how he makes his moves, where his feeding areas are, and especially his bedding grounds, you can take advantage of that knowledge as much as two and three weeks later when the hunting seasons commence.

What do you look for when you're scouting during the rut? Anything, practically anything! High activity areas are excellent places to start. Look for large numbers of scrapes or rubs in a small area. Then look for trails leading in and out of the area. Follow the trails, especially the heavily used ones!

Sometimes those trails lead directly to feeding or bedding areas. Sometimes you lose them and have to locate another high-use area with loads of rutting behavior apparent. By the time you locate three of four high-activity rutting grounds within a fairly small area, and follow the deer trails that lead to and from them, you'll have at least one bedding area and one feeding area pinpointed, probably several for each.

It was while scouting during the rutting period, hunting grouse, that I discovered the saddle mentioned at the beginning of all this. First I discovered a high-use rut area on the northwest side of the hill. The tracks led up over the saddle, to a feeding area of crab apples adjacent to a small winter wheat field.

On the southeast side of the saddle I later found another hotspot where a rutting buck or two had torn things up. I

Deer signs you discover while hunting and scouting during the rut can lead you to a post-rut buck.

followed the trail out of there. It, too, led up across the saddle, then down the other side in a different direction, to a cutover of about three acres. This, I discovered in bird season, was the bedding grounds of at least two bucks and several does, as well as a fair smattering of grouse. Further, the saddle was a patchwork of tracks that came over the hills in both directions. That year the scouting was easy.

Saddles, in mountain or extremely hilly terrain, tend to offer excellent spots for the whitetail hunter to take up his watch. It was so cold that morning that I was only minutes away from climbing out of my tree stand and sneak hunting to the 3-acre cutover, hoping to ease up on a buck already in his bed, and at the same time warming my freezing toes and fingers a tad. It was a good secondary game plan, but an unnecessary one that year.

Signs that the rut is on the wane are scrapes that may go for days without being revisited, a lack of freshness to the scars on a rubbed sapling and embattled shrubs which are beginning to look quite peaked. This is when putting the pieces of the whitetail's puzzle together becomes more difficult. What do you do then?

Bucks recently over the peak rut period can be brought back to a high level of sexual behavior by you, the hunter. One way to get bucks rutting again is through the use of scents. Drop fresh estrus doe in every old scrape you can find.

In many instances you'll be able to start bucks rutting again by doing this. Then the bucks will move around more, leaving lots of sign and tracks that you can then follow, in hopes of zeroing in on bedding grounds, feeding spots, high-use trails, etc. Remember, no matter what period of the fall you hunt deer, scouting is a key to consistent success. Those who live in states where the deer season occurs after the rut has been in full swing can have a definite advantage come opening morning—if they've done their homework and discovered where the bucks are living and how they get from A to B to C, and so forth.

If you haven't done any pre-season scouting at all, and you're faced with what to do opening morning, you're destined to bank on luck and little else. The little else you can do to improve your chances centers around scents, or mainly the lack of it—human, that is. However, all hunters can and should take advantage of this one. Your clothing, from underwear on out, should be freshly laundered. I take a shower the morning of the hunt, rather than the evening before, washing with an odor eliminating soap. Actually, I wash as all my deer hunting clothes in this type of odor eliminating soap. You can never be too clean!

Many hunters swear by heavily scented masking odors, but my experiences with them have tended to spook more deer than not. Instead, I like to use a scent that's natural and deer oriented. Around the stand, it's a good idea to sprinkle this type of scent on eye-height limbs, maybe position a soaked cotton ball or two in the crotch of a tree at a similar level. Sometimes I completely surround my stand with these scent pots. Hopefully, then, any approaching bucks will whiff the scent of my imaginary deer before smelling me, and by then I'll try to have a high-stepping, fast-expand bullet placed between his ribs or through his shoulder.

In more and more states, blackpowder and bowhunting seasons are being scheduled for periods after the gun seasons. Sometimes these take place four to eight weeks after the peak of the rut! My suggestions for scouting during the rut don't have as much merit for these later deer seasons. Further, if gun seasons take place in between, the habits of at least some of the bucks will be altered. However, with fewer hunters afield in these later seasons, the critters often go back to their normal life patterns, which, unfortunately for those who did a lot of scouting during the rut, may not be all that close to the movement patterns they used back then.

Most of the time though, high-use areas are high-use areas. If the habitat is good, the deer will tend to be there. If anything, expect the deer, especially the bucks, to hop up in even thicker thickets. In most instances these extra thick hiding spots need not be very big at all in later winter. If it's big enough for a pickup truck it's more than big enough for any buck that ever made the record book.

Such super thick areas are excellent for the bowhunter to set up a tree stand. He should, however do this several days before the late-season opener, thus giving any mossy horn in residence time to calm down and forget the intrusion to his private bailiwick.

The blackpowder hunter may be able to sneak hunt a thicket of the type I'm describing, but two or three muzzle-loader partners will have an infinitely better chance of scoring when they surround such a place's escape routes. The muzzle-loading hunter going it alone will be better off taking the bowhunter's approach to this situation—getting his subtle tree stand positioned several days prior to the late-season opening.

This past season I again hunted a saddle, the easiest access the deer had in moving from one side of the ridge to the other.

Paradoxically, this time it was on the saddle itself that I found more than a dozen scrapes, scraped saplings galore, plus scads of embattled shrubs. It was colder than ever, especially 16-feet up in my tree stand, and I had to shiver up there well into the afternoon before a six-pointer trotted through. The 100-grain bullet from my .240 Wthby knocked him against one of the saplings he himself had probably rubbed. My success again had to be attributed to pre-season, during the rut scouting.

7

Early Birds Get Their Bucks

by Jeff Murray

"*T*o everything there is a season, and a time to every purpose under heaven."

Indeed, the outdoor writer of biblical times knew what he was talking about. Knowing when to do something is as important as knowing how to do it. Since becoming a year-round deer hunter, I have come to appreciate the value of this great lesson. I bet I've learned as much about whitetail out of the traditional hunting season as in it. In fact, I know of no better way to zero in on a big buck in unfamiliar territory than by scouting in the spring of the year. But I'm getting way ahead of myself.

No doubt, the name of the game is scouting. Any accomplished hunter will tell you that there's a direct relationship between the amount of deer sign near a particular stand and the number of deer that are likely to pass by it. Fall scouting is very important for fine-tuning your game plan and drawing up alternative strategies. Yet fall is not the time to begin your search for a specific animal, or learning the lay of the land in new areas. The bulk of your homework should be done in the springtime.

Since the best way to kill a mature buck is during the rutting season, rut sign is what we need to read most accurately. That's why a majority of hunters scuffle about in the fall, looking for fresh rubs, scrapes, droppings and beds. Now, if what I'm saying is true,

This buck will leave a lot of sign for scouting hunters to find in the spring. Old rut sign is still visible, for example.

there appears to be a contradiction here: How can old rut sign be of any value?

There are plenty of hard-to-argue-with reasons why you should seriously consider adding spring scouting to your whitetail game plan.

Spring is a great time to concentrate on what you're doing—looking for prospective ambush sites, not trying to fill a tag. The fall hunting season is the time to hunt, not half-hunt and half-scout (granted, improvising is often necessary).

Spring affords the average hunter more time. He's not trying to squeeze a few duck, pheasant and grouse outings into an already overcommitted calendar. Scouting, if it's to be done effectively, takes time. You need to pay attention to details. You must make good decisions after analyzing all the information you assemble. You can't pull it off if you're in a hurry; undivided attention to seemingly insignificant details will pay great dividends.

Springtime gives the hunter the best "track record," making accurate interpretations much easier. Right after snow melt, the leaves on the ground are compacted and the trees are bare. Visibility is excellent, making rub hunting a breeze. Scraping areas also become readily discernible in the barren landscape. Better yet, deer trails—even the minor ones used more frequently by bucks—are most obvious this time of year.

This can be a tremendous advantage. For example you might be able to see why a specific scrape was always visited from a certain vantage point. Or, a "secondary " trail, upon further examination, might prove to be anything but secondary. All in all, springtime gives the astute observer a definite advantage over any other time of the year.

Another clue, one that's within reach only during spring forays, can shed a lot of light on the subject of big buck scouting. Antlers shed on the forest floor can tell you as much about an area's potential as the racks that are on the deer the following fall. Naturally, shed antlers are easier to locate than the deer themselves, which really gives the enterprising spring scouter an upper hand.

What's so important about sheds? Many things. For starters, they can tell you plenty about the animal that dropped them. Obviously, a big, thick set ought to quicken your pulse. You can be pretty sure the sheds are from a deer that made it through the last hunting season, and chances are the buck's rack is going to be in a similar condition the following fall. Any sheds you find in the spring are almost certain to have been cast off a few months earlier; they're quickly chewed up by a host of rodents, and they rarely last past the first season. Also, if you do your spring scouting right, scouring the same pockets that cough up sheds year after year, you can easily see how old a buck is, and how well he is developing.

This is especially helpful for trophy hunters. By collecting racks from the same buck year after year, you'll know if the deer is in its prime. If so, the tines and the main beam will be larger and wider each successive year. You'll also know whether it's an older animal on the decline, because the rack will diminish in size and likely add small, non-typical points.

Collecting racks over the years from several distinct areas will also give you an indication of the overall health of different deer populations. If one area is laced year after year with many wrist-thick, multi-tined sheds, while another one only yields scrawny sheds, which one would be better to hunt in the fall? Genetics and soil types are the two most influential factors affecting antler development, and I know of no better way to cut through all the whitetail red tape and find out where and why. As alluded to earlier, this could be the most effective way to scout unfamiliar woods to determine their big-buck densities.

There is one more very important detail that shed antlers can give the spring scouter—where bucks bed. As you can see, sheds can be a mighty big clue, but the ability to pinpoint whitetail bedding sites must rank at the top. Sheds are most likely dropped within hollering distance of the buck's main bedding area, and if you find the sheds, you've got the bedroom pretty well established. And, if you know where a buck beds, you've got him cornered.

Why? Because that's the hub of his activity. Like the spokes of a wheel, all his comings and goings will generally emerge from this center. It's that simple.

So, to find sheds, look for prospective bedding cover. In agricultural lands, scour the river bottoms, woodlots and ribbons of high ground associated with willow and cattail swamps. In the deep woods, thickets fairly close to food supplies are your best bet. Pockets of second-growth aspen, tag alder, cedar swamp and swamp islands are prime targets —especially if alfalfa fields or slashings are within close proximity.

Be sure to arrive on the scene as soon as the snow melts. Sheds don't last long.

Hunting shed antlers can be almost as exciting as the real thing. Hopefully, you'll end up with a lasting memento as a reward for your efforts, one that continually reminds you of the animal that grew it. Over the summer, however, your imagination might get the best of you, so don't get carried away and lock yourself into the area that your biggest shed came from.

Greg Miller, a Wisconsin big-buck hunter, has learned that collecting sheds is very addictive for another reason—it can lead to some critical discoveries.

"When I find a shed," Miller told me, "I always scour the immediate vicinity to see of there is a reason why the buck happened to drop the antler(s) in that particular spot. Many times, the terrain doesn't look any different than the surrounding country, and I'd probably pass it over in favor of the next ridge or valley. But after I get the "magnifying glass" out, something usually catches my eye."

That "something" is usually a rub line, which Miller likes to incorporate into this stand placement strategy. Without the sheds, many of his most productive rub lines would have gone unnoticed.

A similar occurrence happened to me a few years ago. I was fairly new to the game of shed-finding, and hadn't quite learned the principle of really combing the immediate ground where a shed turns up. What happened? The ensuing fall I kicked up a nine-point buck from the edge of a tangled tag alder thicket a stone's throw away from where the shed came from the previous spring. I know it was the same buck, because I got a good look at the rack as the buck literally leaped in front of me. The shed matched the buck's unusually upright rack. To make matters worse, last fall I saw the buck again, confirming my hunch that this was indeed, this main bedding area. Wait 'til next year. …

Spring and early summer are also good times to get a visual on whitetails, but as the leaves pop out, you're really handicapped by the emerging vegetation. Also, field-scanning with binoculars is less productive at this time of year than later on in the fall, because of the abundance of forage within more forested tracts; deer still come to feed, but most fields just don't offer the menu of a woodlot or forest opening. Besides, the security of ample cover is definitely preferred where available. However, this doesn't rule out all summer scouting.

Instead of looking for deer hides, take a good look at how the landscape is laid out. In farmland this is extremely important. Farmers rotate their crops annually, leaving some areas fallow and planting others with deer-attracting corn, oats, alfalfa, soybeans or milo. The layout of croplands, in turn, will affect deer movement patterns the following fall. It's a domino effect, and the sooner you get a handle on it, the more time you'll have for going over details in the deer's core area(s).

There is a place for summer, but it's much less significant. I like to keep an eye out on new logging operations. They can have a devastating effect in some extreme cases. A buddy, for instance, built a tree stand that produced a nice buck for three consecutive years. Then you could say he got complacent. He didn't do any fall scouting, and it really cost him. On opening day he was flabbergasted to find his favorite aspen tree in the middle of a mile-wide clearcut. As a cruel joke, the loggers left his scaffold intact, for all to see!

Scouting is hardly a panacea. You still have to execute, but scouting will do for you what nothing else will.

8

Post-Season Scouting In The North

by Greg Miller

 W hite-tailed deer hunters are a very curious bunch indeed. For eight months they are some of the most dedicated, hard-working hunters you'll find anywhere.

Still, for all their dedication, eight months is four too few. In fact, what many deer hunters continue to overlook might be one of the most beneficial scouting periods.

From late spring to the very end of the open season, most serious hunters can be found afield working hard at improving their chances for success. These individuals run themselves ragged, searching for shed antlers, scouting, observing and doing whatever else it takes to get within range of massive, mature bucks.

For most hunters, however, the end of deer season means it's time to stow away hunting gear, kick back by the fireplace, rest and reflect on seasons gone by. Unfortunately, they are missing out on one of the best times to be in the woods scouting for seasons yet to come.

The toughest part of my job as both a writer and deer hunting educator has been to convince people of the importance of post-season scouting. Yet, I can understand why many hunters are hesitant to head right back into the woods at season's end. You see, at one time I was a skeptic too.

So what's the great advantage of returning to the deer woods immediately upon the close of the season? Simply put, at this time whitetails are in what I've come to call "strict survival patterns." What this means is that they are still in the identical bedding, traveling and feeding routines as during the open season. Obviously, therefore, the information you gather during post-season scouting forays can be of immense help once deer feel the pressure during future seasons. But be forewarned, successful post-season scouting entails more than just a leisurely stroll through the woods.

I think it's important that you approach your post-season scouting with a definite game plan. First of all, target a specific area in which to scout. Second, go into that area with the intention of finding out all you can about the buck(s) that reside there. Third, and most important, search out stand sites you're confident will afford you your best opportunity during the next season.

Of course, all this sounds a bit more simple than it really is. Still, you can accomplish these goals without expending too much energy or time. Quite honestly, you should be able to thoroughly cover several different areas in just a few days.

I prefer to concentrate the majority of my post-season scouting efforts in familiar areas. To me, nothing is worse than spending valuable hours walking through an area only to find the place has absolutely no potential. And that's exactly what can happen when you head into unknown turf. The name of the game is to get a lot accomplished in a relatively short period of time. So, if at all possible, stick to familiar ground!

My hunting partners and I have hit upon a rather effective pattern for pinpointing buck bedding areas on post-season scouting trips. First of all, we simply eliminate those places we know bucks just won't use as daytime sanctuaries (open hardwood ridges, pastured woodlots, etc. ...). Instead we concentrate on those spots that we've come to recognize as being virtual buck havens.

Expansive briar thickets, blown-down areas, thick pine groves, abandoned home-sites, swamps or any other dense, impenetrable cover probably warrant a closer look. Narrowing down the possibilities means a lot less leg work. And, believe me, this can be an important factor when you're searching for the hideouts of several big bucks.

After we've selected some habitat with big-buck holding potential, we walk right through the middle of any and all suspected bedding areas. Our intention from the beginning is to jump the buck(s) we think might be holed up in such spots. If we're successful, we pay close attention to where the buck runs when jumped.

Obviously, these are the routes he prefers to use when he feels threatened. (Valuable information should you decide to make a small, well-organized deer drive through that area next season.)

After the buck has departed, we spend some time attempting to learn all we can about his bedding area. Where exactly does he lie? How does he enter/exit the bedding area? And where would you stand your best chance of ambushing the buck as he's coming or going?

If possible, we'll take the time right then and there to establish several stand sites that allow us to exploit what we've learned about that particular buck. Then, in most cases, we'll stay away until it's time to come back and hunt next year.

Even not-so-experienced deer hunters can attest that hunting pressure drastically alters the feeding habits of whitetails. Not only do they often change the times and ways in which they approach/exit feeding areas, they frequently select different places to feed.

Secluded oak ridges, isolated crop attractants and thick browse areas are just a few of the places whitetails will use as in-season food sources. Again, returning to the woods right on the heels of the season should enable you to pinpoint these feeding areas.

During a recent season, I shot a heavy-horned 11-point buck in Wisconsin. All told, I had spent the better part of two seasons hunting that particular deer. In addition, I had invested untold hours scouting. Without a doubt, the most important information was accumulated during some rather intense post-season scouting sessions.

A substantial snow cover enabled me to determine the preferred routes used by the buck to travel about his range. Secondly, I discovered where he was feeding and watering. But most importantly, I learned exactly where the big deer was hiding out during daylight hours.

The next step was to establish stand sites at numerous key locations. Some of these stands were positioned to take advantage of travel corridors the buck used most often. I also prepared several ambush points in strategic locations on the very edge of a small tamarack swamp. Post-season scouting trips revealed the buck was utilizing the swamp as his bedding sanctuary.

I hunted the trophy deer off and on the next year during our lengthy bow season. Although I saw him on several occasions, he never ventured near enough for a shot. It wasn't until the fifth day of our nine-day gun-deer season that the buck made a mistake. He wandered out of his bedding area during the mid-morning hours for a bite to eat. The range was a mere 35 yards, which made it an easy shot with my scoped .270 Win.

Many deer hunters here in the North place great importance upon having snow to assist them in their post-season scouting. But to be quite honest, I don't look at a lack of snow as a hindrance. Actually, it could be viewed as a decided advantage.

Granted, snow cover can tell you a lot about the current travel routines of whitetails in a specific area. And actually tracking deer can help you discover the exact location of preferred bedding and feeding areas. Such information certainly is extremely beneficial. Truth is, however, there are times when I'd love to be afforded the luxury of an "open winter." Though snow cover can tell you a lot about the current activities of whitetails, it can also cover up one heck of a lot of fresh deer sign. And in many cases here in Wisconsin, I'm then forced to wait until late spring before I'll be able to read and decipher that sign.

In my opinion, the biggest negative about having snow is it completely covers up scrape sign. I base a lot of my pre-rut hunting strategies around the locations of rubs and scrapes. Now, I will occasionally rely solely on one or the other of these visual signposts for stand placement. However, I feel a lot better when I can concentrate my efforts in areas where bucks are both rubbing and scraping.

Snow also hides that crucial sign you need to determine exactly which runways might have seen the most use during the late pre-rut. And because of the bright white background, it can be quite difficult spotting rubs against snow.

Some of us here in the North have to worry about getting too much snow. (And trust me, there have been plenty of winters like that in my memory.) When you get snow depths of more than 30 inches, I'm afraid any sort of post-season scouting becomes nothing more than an exercise in futility.

Sure, it is possible to return to the woods after snow-melt in the spring to search for scrapes and other bits of previous fall deer sign, but I'd rather dedicate those precious weeks in the spring to exploring new country and searching for shed antlers.

This post-season period is also an excellent time to figure out a "problem buck." I think a lot of hunters know what I'm talking about here—a deer that just seems to give us the slip at every turn, and is always one step ahead of us.

Heading right back into the woods immediately after the season ends is the absolute best way to increase your knowledge about such animals. The great thing about scouting now is you don't have to be quite as careful as during the open season. You can walk anywhere, jump deer intentionally, take chances with the wind, etc.

Remember, that buck will have nearly a whole year to forget about these few bad experiences. In the meantime, you might learn just enough about him to put the odds in your favor next season— like exactly what he does when the heat is on.

Going back into the woods right after season often can provide you with information needed to determine exactly which bucks survived and which didn't. Fresh tracks, scrapes, rubs and actual sightings all can be used to confirm the presence of bucks you'll have the opportunity to pursue again next season. On the other hand, gut piles and "drag-trails" can substantiate rumors you've heard regarding the harvesting of certain big bucks from specific areas.

So if post-season scouting is such a good thing, why don't more deer hunters take advantage of the excellent opportunities available at this time? Well, it's my guess that many just might be suffering from severe burn-out by season's end. Three or four straight months of extended scouting trips, hundreds of hours spent in cramped tree stands, too many all-day hunts and a severe shortage of sleep can take a toll on even the most dedicated hunter.

So reward yourself. Take a day or two off. Then get back in the woods and figure out how that big buck outsmarted you last week. It's a 12-month game, and it's not over yet.

9

Post-Season Scouting
In The South

by Larry Weishuhn

Slipping from the dense cover of the dry creek bed, the buck stopped and checked his backtrail. Carefully, he surveyed the area, then eased forward. All the while he took full advantage of what available cover there was between him and the next thicket. I watched his every movement through 10X binoculars. He never knew I was there.

I had hunted this wise, mature buck the past two seasons. Yet, I had never seen him while I was hunting. In years past I had seen bucks like him become completely nocturnal after the slightest bit of hunting pressure. Was this such a buck?

Taking such bucks often requires learning as much as you can about the deer, starting immediately after the season closes, and being persistent.

The hunting season had been closed for only a week when I ventured into the haunts of the old buck. I hoped to learn as much as possible of the deer's hunting season behavior. Actually, the purpose of the trip to the area was twofold. The property held an abundance of wild hogs and I intended to add some pork to our winter larder. While doing so, I hoped to unravel a few big buck mysteries.

During my 40 years of hunting whitetails, I have determined the best way to learn about bucks and where they go during the hunting season is to continue "hunting" them throughout the year, especially right after the season closes. In hunting seminars, I have often mentioned, "I hunt deer year-round!" This statement is usually met with a few looks of surprise, some of condemnation and even a few questions from game wardens.

Before they haul me off to the hoosegow, let me explain. Perhaps it would be better to say I "scout" immediately after the deer season closes and continue scouting throughout the year.

Deer return to their normal routines after the end of the hunting season. While they are still wary, they do not act nearly as "hunter-wise" as they did a few weeks earlier. After the season closes, deer also do not seem to be quite as concerned about a human's presence in their habitat. They seem more interested in filling their rumens and surviving the winter than they do in eluding humans.

Unlike in the North, where whitetails "yard up" during the winter, Southern whitetails tend to live in the same general area throughout the year. This makes winter scouting and relating findings to fall activities considerably easier than in some other areas.

During my winter scouting trips, I maintain a journal of deer sign and activities on the places I hunt. This journal includes several maps of the area, including a topographical map, an aerial survey map and several small hand-drawn maps of specific areas on the property.

About a week following the closing of the deer season, after the deer have settled down, I again head to the woods. Once again deer are doing the same things in the same places they did the latter part of the season, only now more openly.

The deer sign I look for during these winter scouting trips includes rubs and scrapes. Both are still readily visible. Both can be visited and inspected without your having to worry about leaving an abundance of human scent in the area. During the season, leaving much scent around a rub or scrape might spook a big, mature buck or cause him to change his daily routine. After the season has closed, he will not pay as much attention to human scent left in his home range as he did earlier.

Using maps, I carefully mark where each of the scrapes was found, not only to indicate their presence and abundance, but also to help me determine patterns established by deer. Where appropriate, I sketch small maps of the specific area showing trails, individual plants, prevailing wind directions and possible ambush sites downwind from the scrape in preparation for the next hunting season. I pay particular attention not only to their location, but whether or not they were active in past years, if I have that information from having previously winter-scouted the area. Some scrapes on properties I hunt have been active each of the past eight years.

During my winter scouting trips, I try to determine if there is a particular pattern to the scrapes. Are they laid out in somewhat of a line or semi-circle? Does it appear scrapes are found primarily on certain sides of trees (under overhanging limbs)? Do the scrapes show anything about which way the deer normally travels relative to prevailing fall and early winter winds? Is there anything peculiar or distinct about tracks that appear in the pawed out place in the scrape?

I try to learn as much as I can about the scrapes and the deer that make and use them during the breeding season. Spending the same amount of time around these scrapes during the fall would only tend to alert the mature bucks in the area and make them change their patterns.

Rubs indicate the presence of bucks. Scrapes can be, and sometimes are, made by does. However, I have never seen a doe making a rub! Some rubs are used only one time and never again visited. These are normally "frustration" rubs, where a buck takes out his aggravation on the nearest available shrub. Other rubs are used again and again, by the same buck and also by other bucks. Primarily, when scouting immediately after the season, I look for rubs that show a lot of use. On my maps and in my journal I will make note of all kinds of rubs, but I will put more emphasis on those that show considerable use, and especially those that seem to have been used year after year. These are easily spotted because they show signs of having been rubbed in the past, where the tree has been trying to "heal" itself, as well as current gouge and rub marks. I pay particular attention to the size of the tree rubbed, the species of the tree, size of the rub, and the side of the tree the rub is on. In some instances deer keep on rubbing their antlers until only a few days before they are cast. Thus, even late in the winter there still appear to be fresh rubs.

Generally, the bigger the tree rubbed, the bigger the buck making it. Pay particular attention to the side of the tree a buck rubs on because it gives some indication as to the direction he normally travels. If you find more than one rub along a trail (a good place to find both rubs and scrapes) and the second is on the same side of the tree as the first rub you found, it indicates which direction the buck normally travels. This will help you determine where to set up the following hunting season. If the rubbed tree shows indications of having been rubbed during previous years, all the more reason to hunt that area.

Checking the surface of the rub gives you some indication about the surface of the buck's antlers. If the rubbed surface of the tree is smooth, chances are pretty good the bucks antlers will have a smooth surface. If the rub's surface is grooved, chances are good the buck's antlers will be gnarly.

If there are limbs, twigs or brush on the opposite side of where the rub was made, you can get some idea as to the length of a buck's tines or even the spread, by where these were dinged or broken.

All these bits of information are recorded in my journals and illustrated on the maps accompanying them. If I happen to see bucks while out gathering this "data," those sightings are recorded along with where the deer were seen and what they were doing.

Winter is a critical time for most deer, especially in terms of available food. While scouting during the winter, I make every attempt to learn what deer are eating. In some instances, I might watch deer browsing. At other times, I might be able to determine what deer eat by looking at the tips of vegetation that shows signs of being chewed on. I record these sites and identify the plants.

Throughout much of the South, acorns are a favorite, as are persimmons, and other hard and soft mast crops. However, by the middle of the hunting season these mast crops are generally very limited or completely gone. Then what do deer eat? Some of that information can be learned by consulting a local wildlife biologist. During the hunting season, opening up the rumen of harvested deer is a sure way to learn what deer are eating.

A few years ago I hunted in north-central Alabama. I knew two of the favorite deer foods were white oak acorns and beechnuts. However, by the time I finally got to hunt, those choice tidbits were gone. Thankfully, I had scouted the area the previous winter and noticed there were three areas on the property that had an abundance of honeysuckle, which had been browsed quite heavily. Thus, I knew where to start hunting.

Throughout most of the South, whitetails retain their antlers until the early spring. Finding sheds, regardless of when they are found, can lead the hunter to deer, especially if the sheds are fairly fresh, or not over a year old. Sheds definitely indicate the presence of bucks.

During the past 20 years I have taken numerous mature bucks within less than 400 yards of where I found their sheds. Some bucks were taken less than 100 yards of where their shed antlers were found. During any scouting trip, I always look for cast antlers and carefully make notes of where they were found. Many other hunters have told me they consistently take bucks close to where they find sheds.

For the true whitetail aficionado, the deer season never really ends. The day the hunting season closes, that's the day scouting season begins. Not only does winter scouting provide information for future hunts, it brings the hunter closer to deer and helps one understand and appreciate how the whitetail behaves throughout the year.

If you are not scouting during the winter, you are missing some truly unique opportunities! In fact, you might be passing up your best chance of taking that bruiser buck next season.

Field Judging &
The Moment of Truth

1

Five Seconds To Success

by Larry Weishuhn

A mature, hunter-wise white-tailed buck seldom gives a hunter more than five seconds to spot him, evaluate his antlers and age, estimate the distance and make a killing shot. That doesn't seem like very much time, does it? It isn't!

If you are interested in taking mature bucks you better not expect more than five seconds. How you use those precious seconds can spell the difference between success and failure.

The first step in taking a good whitetail is hunting areas where mature bucks exist. However, hunting the right areas doesn't guarantee you'll see big bucks. You need to know where and how to look for deer. Too often we look for calendar poses and expect to see deer standing in the open. Rarely will this happen. It is far better to expect to see only parts of deer, like the twitch of an ear or a tail, sunlight glinting off of an antler, or the dark spots of a deer's nose or eyes.

As soon as you see a deer, concentrate on its head to quickly identify whether it is a buck or doe. If antlers are present, try to determine the number of points, tine length, main beam length, mass and spread. Some hunters are interested in number of points, some in spread, others in the overall size of the rack, and still others in the Boone and Crockett score. I want a mature deer with antlers that please me.

While looking at the buck's head, determine if both sides of the rack are present, then check if both sides are fairly equal in size. The next step is to count the number of points off the main beam. Look at one side of the rack. If the main beam has a brow tine and one primary tine, the buck is likely a 6-point. If there is a brow tine and two primary points coming off the main beam, the buck is likely an 8-point. For each additional primary point, the total increases by two—three primaries, 10-point; four primaries, 12-point.

After you have quickly estimated the number of typical points, look for any "kicker" or nontypical points. To me, kicker points add to the beauty of a rack, but beauty is in the eye of the beholder.

If you are interested in B&C scores, you can quickly estimate a rack's gross score by knowing a few simple, fairly standard measurements on a deer's head. Compare these measurements to estimate tine length, main beam length (which comprise the greater part of the B&C scores), circumference and inside spread.

These comparison measurements include the length of a deer's ear (normally 8 inches from tip to where it attaches to the neck and 6 inches from the opening of the ear to the tip); eye to nose

A quick glance reveals this buck should be about an 8-point, but you need another angle to confirm it. Sometimes, though, you simply have to gamble or your five seconds runs out.

(from the forward edge of the eye to the tip of the nose), which averages about 7 to 8 inches; ear tip to ear tip spread when the ears are in an erect position, about 16 to 17 inches (although it varies from region to region); and the circumference of the deer's eye, which is about 4 inches. With these "knowns" you can quickly estimate the B&C gross score.

If you are interested in a mature buck, quickly look past the antlers at the deer's face, neck and body. Young bucks have relatively tight skin about their face and their muscles are not yet fully developed. In addition, young bucks have skinny necks during the fall breeding season. Mature bucks, those 4 years and older have more fully developed bodies. In the fall their necks are swollen. They have a fair amount of loose skin about their face, including loose skin or jowls hanging under their jaw line. The mature buck might be slightly pot-bellied and his legs might appear too short for his body. Also, most mature bucks have darkly-stained hocks during the breeding season.

For example, let's say we have spotted a buck. His neck is swollen past the width of his jaw. He has jowls and his hocks are darkly stained. A quick check tells you the buck has both antlers present, with three primary tines, and a brow tine on each side. To begin the B&C gross score guess, estimate the total inches of antler present on one side. It appears the brow tine is half as long as the buck's ear, or about 4 inches. The back tine is as long as the overall length of the buck's ear, or about 8 inches. The next tine forward is approximately the same length. The front tine is about the same length as the brow tine, or 4 inches. The main beam is about three times the length of the eye to nose measurement, or about 21 inches. Each of the four circumference measurements are equal to the circumference of the deer's eye, about 4 inches. The base circumference is a little larger, and the front measurement between the third and fourth point is a little smaller, but it appears the measurement averages about 4 inches for a total of 16 inches (B&C measurements include four circumference measurements on both sides).

Quickly add the numbers 4+8+8+4+21+16 for a total of 61 inches. Double that figure, because the other side is approximately equal, for a total of 122. The buck turns to look at you. The inside spread of the main beams is just beyond the erect forward ears, or about 17 inches. Add the accumulated measurements of both sides of the rack to the inside spread and the gross estimated score is 139 B&C points.

Practice on mounted deer heads during the off-season. After a while you will learn to quickly get an impression of what a rack will score.

If the buck interests you, you must next estimate the range. If you are hunting with a bow, your range is extremely limited. If you shoot a blackpowder rifle, shotgun or revolver you are limited to about 100-yard shots. If you shoot a rifle or one of the single-shot handguns chambered for the rifle cartridges, the opportunity for longer shots exists. With my rifles and handguns, I prefer to use variable scopes in the 3.5-10X range with good light-gathering abilities, and duplex style crosshairs.

With my Simmons scopes, if the power setting is on 5, at 100 yards, a large deer standing broadside is bracketed between the broad portion of the crosshairs from the front of the chest to the backside of the rump. If the deer is bracketed in this manner or bigger, I immediately know the deer is 100 yards or less away. If the deer is 300 yards away it will be bracketed between the broad portion of the crosshairs with the power setting on 8X. Practice at the rifle range using life-sized deer targets to see where your variable scope "brackets" a deer.

By knowing where your rifle is sighted in and where a particular load will strike a target at varying distances you greatly increase your odds of taking a big buck. I shoot from a solid rest if at all possible! Even though I have the chance to see hundreds of big bucks each year, they still make me excited, and I want all the help I can get to make a killing shot.

Lots of things to think about and do in just five seconds? Perhaps, but when you're talking big bucks, the clock is definitely ticking!

2

Field Judging Trophy Whitetail

by Chuck Adams

*T*he white-tailed deer is every man's big-game animal. More whitetails are harvested in North America than any other species, and populations continue to rise from the Pacific to the Atlantic. At present, white-tailed deer are hunted in 47 of the 50 states in the U.S., plus every province in Canada and most parts of Old Mexico. If you wish to try for whitetails, you can travel far or you can stay very close to home.

From a trophy standpoint, however, certain areas are clearly superior to others. Many sportsmen dream about bagging wall-hanging white-tailed bucks, yet continue to hunt year after year in non-trophy locales. Some places, like parts of Pennsylvania, Michigan and Texas, are heavily hunted and nearly devoid of bucks over 3½ years old. Consequently, large-racked trophies are scarce as hen's teeth. Other habitats, like the Florida Keys and Anticosti Island, apparently lack the genetic potential or proper forage to produce bucks with truly giant antlers.

Impressive white-tailed bucks are harvested in many, many places, but you must do your homework to find areas with proper feed, genetics and trophy management. Some places, like South Texas, Alberta, Saskatchewan, northwestern Montana, Minnesota, Iowa, Illinois, Kansas, Indiana, Missouri and Wisconsin, are genuine hotspots for giant racks. Others, like New York, Maine and Georgia, produce nice bucks in specific locales with a combination of light hunting pressure, good nutrition and time-tested genetics.

If you want a big buck, don't spin your wheels where forkhorns and small 8-points are the rule. Go where the big boys live!

There are more than 30 subspecies of whitetails on our continent. These vary in physical stature from the 80-pound Florida Key deer to Northern whitetails scaling more than 300 pounds.

Nonetheless, all whitetails have distinctive traits in common. In the fall, their faces and brows are uniformly brown-gray except for a white band behind the nose and white circles around the eyes. Ears are relatively short compared to body size, averaging 18 inches from tip to tip.

The tail is equally distinctive—a long, fluffy appendage with a topside of gray-brown and an underside of stark white. When running, a whitetail usually lifts this "flag" and wags it back and forth—a white signal issued by no other deer. In Western and Midwestern states where whitetails and mule deer are hunted concurrently, these physical traits set the whitetail apart.

The average whitetail's antlers are also unique, although nontypical racks can defy ready identification. Main beams sprout from the head, curve upward and backward at first, then jut dramatically forward above the nose. Whitetail racks do not normally double-branch (bifurcate) like those on blacktails and mule deer. Instead, all tines rise from a common main beam like candles in a row. Eyeguards tend to be longer than those on other species of deer.

On average, a mature white-tailed buck of 4½ to 6½ years old carries a total of 10 typical tines—one eyeguard, one main beam, and three upright points per side. Such a deer is called a 10 point. A few bucks never progress beyond four points per side and such 8-points can be immense at middle age. A nice non-record 10-point whitetail rack will spread to the eartips when viewed from the front. From the side, main beams will project to the back of the nose. Eyeguards will vary between 3 and 8 inches long, and other points will measure 4 to 10 inches long. Mass will not be eye-stopping compared to length of beams. Such a buck will carry main beams of 19 to 23 inches long. Antler bases will measure between 3 and 5½ inches in circumference. A deer of this caliber will score between 120 and 150 Boone & Crockett points—a definite cut above the norm. Most such bucks will also exceed the Pope & Young bowhunting minimum of 125.

A genuine Boone & Crockett whitetail is distinctive. To exceed the minimum all-time record-book score of 170, a buck must carry a massive rack with extra-long beams and a colossal spread. Main beams will measure 24 to 30 inches long and extend beyond the tip of the nose when viewed from the side. Antler mass will be substantial, with main beams measuring four to six inches in circumference at the base. Antlers will spread one to five inches beyond each eartip, and primary tines will rise high above the head.

He's not Boone & Crockett, but he's still a tremendous 8-point buck. Taken with a bow, he would easily make the Pope & Young record book.

Two typical whitetails in the B&C list have inside main beam spreads of more than 30 inches, but a 23-inch inside spread is par for the course with record-book contenders. Tines will commonly measure 10 or 12 inches long. Eyeguards can be quite long, too, sometimes exceeding 12 inches on each side. Many typical B&C

bucks carry more than three upright tines forward of the eyeguards, increasing the total number of tines to 12 or more. Such racks should be symmetrical with no major nontypical drop tines, "cheaters" jutting to one side, multiple eyeguards or similar gingerbread. Few hunters will pass up a giant whitetail with non-typical tines, but such a deer can miss B&C as a direct result.

Any typical whitetail scoring over 150 B&C points is impressive on the hoof. To an experienced eye, antlers seem to overpower the animal's head at a glance. Rack coloration can be a bit of a fooler, with light-colored antlers appearing larger in dimension yet less massive than they really are. Dark-brown racks tend to appear more massive and smaller in dimension. Only close scrutiny can help you overcome these size-judging pitfalls.

In-depth research shows that most whitetails in the Boone & Crockett list were bagged during the peak rutting period between mid-November and mid-December. A whitetail is one of North America's most skittish creatures, and a mature hatrack buck can be almost impossible to locate before he drops his guard to rut. Modern rut-hunting technology, including use of scents, grunt calls and rattling antlers, can give serious hunters a primary edge at the magic time of year.

In addition, time-tested tactics like snow tracking, deer driving and stand hunting along feeding fields can work well when foliage, hunting pressure and weather are conducive to such ploys.

3

Field Judging
Trophy Coues' Deer

by Chuck Adams

The Coues' deer is a Southwestern whitetail subspecies and is North America's smallest officially recognized antlered trophy. On average, a mature Coues' buck weighs less than 100 pounds and sports a tight, short-tined basket rack that appears almost "cute" compared to antlers on Northern white-tailed deer.

This desert-dwelling animal is in fact a whitetail, but displays physiological characteristics distinctly different from other whitetail strains. For this reason, the Coues' deer is classified as a separate trophy by all major record-keeping organizations.

The Coues' deer inhabits a relatively small range, thriving in arid and semi-arid environments throughout central and southern Arizona, southwestern New Mexico and northern Mexico.

This animal's small size and geographical isolation serves to limit its popularity with nonresident hunters. However, most serious sportsmen who try Coues' deer are instantly and solidly hooked on the experience.

Often referred to as "the gray ghost of the desert," the Coues' deer enjoys a well-deserved reputation for hunting difficulty. Partly because it is unusually alert and skittish, partly because its mouse-gray hide blends perfectly with desert colorations, the Coues' buck is difficult to locate. Add to that some of North America's most inhospitable terrain, and the true trophy Coues' buck quickly stacks up as one of the most difficult antlered trophies to hunt successfully!

Coues' deer are most often spotted from a distance through powerful optics, then stalked and shot in their beds or on the run. Unlike "regular" whitetails, they sometimes bed in semi-open terrain and shun bottomland thickets altogether. Coues' bucks may be small in physical size, but they more than compensate by providing a supreme hunting challenge. Many hunters regard the Coues' deer as our continent's most elusive trophy species.

In some areas, Coues' deer and desert mule deer inhabit the same range. However, these species are distinctly different in appearance, and even beginners should have little difficulty in telling them apart.

Coues' deer are light gray in color, with a uniformly gray head and brow reminiscent of other whitetail subspecies. The muzzle and eyes are lightly ringed with white, and a faint off-white patch is often visible beneath the chin. A Coues' deer's gray-brown tail seems unnaturally long and fluffy, often hanging to the hocks. When this deer runs, it raises its flag in classic whitetail fashion, revealing a stark-white underside.

By comparison, a desert mule deer is darker gray in color, has a brown/black forehead and usually displays distinct, double patches of white on the throat and lower neck. In addition, a desert mule deer has a prominent white rump patch and a short, white, rope-like tail tipped with black. There can be no excuses for confusing these two species of desert deer in the field.

Other physical traits aside, a Coues' bucks' antlers set it sharply apart from desert mules and other official types of deer.

Unlike mule deer, a Coues' buck sports a miniature, whitetail-like basket rack with all tines rising from forward-thrusting, sharply curving main beams. A representative, nonrecord trophy carries three primary tines per side plus eyeguards. This "8-point" rack will appear tiny to whitetail hunters from the East and Midwest. A Coues' deer measures about 17 inches between the eartips, and an average trophy rack will be narrower than the ears. Outside antler spreads of 12 to 14 inches are respectable. When viewed from the side, a trophy Coues' rack extends forward to the bridge of the nose. Main beams measure 13 to 16 inches long. The back tines average 5 to 7 inches long, and the middle tines measure 2 to 4 inches long. Eyeguards vary considerably in length, but tend to be relatively short compared to those on regular whitetail racks. Average eyeguards measure 2 to 3 inches long.

Coues' bucks rarely grow 10-point typical racks. Most often, they remain 8-point throughout their lives. Representative 8-point antlers like those just described seldom appear excessively massive for their size, but heavy-duty versions are sometimes encountered.

Antler coloration varies considerably, but medium gray is the norm. Dark-brown antlers can appear more massive than they actually are.

A good, mature Coues' buck scores between 85 and 100 points on the Boone & Crockett scale. Such a deer makes a fine archery trophy, easily beating the Pope & Young minimum of 60. Most riflemen with Coues' deer experience regard a 95-point deer as excellent—a fine head for the wall. However, such an animal falls noticeably short of the current B&C minimum of 110 points.

A genuine Coues' super-trophy is an animal apart. Time worn advice for trophy hunters is "you'll knows 'em when you sees 'em," and that most assuredly is the case when it comes to record-book Coues'. Such a buck most often sports three primary tines per side plus eyeguards. Beyond this, the similarity with average bucks disappears.

Antlers extend nearly as wide as the eartips, and beams are noticeably longer than the norm. When viewed from the side, a Boone & Crockett rack extends forward to the tip of the nose, and primary tines rise high above the main beam. Back tines are commonly 8 to 10 inches long, and middle tines often exceed 6 inches long. Eyeguards vary considerably in length, but average four to six inches high. Though relatively rare, genuine 5x5 (10-point) Coues' bucks tend to score the best for Boone & Crockett.

An extra tine on each side can boost a trophy score by 10 or 12 points—enough to differentiate a nice 100-point deer from a record-class 110-point buck.

Coues' bucks of B&C size sometimes make the grade on extreme antler mass alone. On average, a mature buck has antler bases 3½ inches in circumference. By contrast, many B&C bucks carry antlers with bases to tips of their beams, and can easily score four to six points more than normal.

Only extensive hunting experience can give you a feel for deer-judging subtleties like antler mass and overall rack dimension.

In decent Coues' buck country, you'll see only two or three branch-antlered deer per day—which means that quick trophy-assessing skill is a hard-earned ability. However, you can short-cut this process by paying strict attention to antler width compared to the ears, and main-beam length compared to head length when viewed from the side. Any animal with ear-wide antlers, back tines 8 inches long, middle tines 6 inches long, and main beams thrusting forward to the nose is a buck to be proud of. If the deer displays even longer tines, an extra typical tine per side, eyeguards over 3 inches long and/or unusually massive antlers, you might be looking at a Boone & Crockett contender!

Giant Coues' bucks have been harvested from all parts of this deer's range, but Arizona dominates in the trophy-production department.

The Coues' deer is not a large animal, but trophy value is subjective. If high challenge and hard hunting appeal to you, this little customer is impossible to beat!

4

Owner's Manual To The Next World Record

by Jim Shockey

Somewhere, sometime in the not-too-distant future, someone is going to tag the new world-record typical white-tailed buck. That buck and the hunter who takes him will gain instant, international notoriety.

Because you are a deer hunter, you could be the one. Far fetched as that may seem, someone will do it, so why not you? If you are the lucky hunter to beat the odds, would you know what to do?

Imagine you're on stand late one fall afternoon. Suddenly, before you appears the most magnificent buck you've ever seen. It happens more quickly than it takes to tell it, thankfully so, because you don't have time to develop buck fever before you aim and the huge animal drops. As you approach, the antlers seem to grow.

By the time you reach down and touch the buck, you're aware it is very special indeed. You are excited, but still manage to remember to tag him immediately. Realizing he is too large for you to drag alone, you head out of the bush and flag down some help. Just as you reach your truck, a vehicle drives down the road. Two hunters stop to chat, and you ask them for help.

A good bit later, as the sun sets, you close the tailgate of your truck. The buck is safe and sound. So for the next hour you relive the hunt with your new friends, explaining in detail how you took the buck with one shot. Happy to vicariously hunt the buck with you, the two hunters congratulate you over and over. Eventually, they part company. You wish them good luck as they drive away, but as their tail lights disappear, you remember that you never did ask their names.

During the hour drive home, you try your best to recall what it was you read about measuring antlers. By the time you back your truck into your garage, it's getting late, but you feel you have to call someone.

You call a friend who says he'll be right over, but since it's poker night, he asks to bring the guys along, too. Of course, the more the merrier.

By the time the guys show up, it's near midnight, but you can't sleep anyway. During the course of the celebration, one of the guys says he knows how to measure your buck for the record book. With bated breath you await the verdict. When it comes you are disappointed. The fellow, puffed out with importance, points his beer at the buck and explains to you that while it is a big buck, it doesn't quite make "the book."

"Oh well," you reason, "it's still big enough to have mounted." But then the guys talk you out of it. It costs a fortune, they tell you. Better to just save the antlers and have them mounted on a plaque.

So the next morning you cut the antlers off and take the carcass to the meat processor. Until the butcher calls a week later, you pretty much forget the whole thing. When you go to pick up the meat and ask for the hide the kid at the counter points to a pile in the corner and says to take whichever one you want or leave it for a donation to the local habitat project. On the same trip, you drop the antlers by the taxidermist.

Still with me? Granted, you might do things differently. Maybe you'd measure the buck yourself or decide to mount the deer in spite of your buddies' advice, but for the most part, the sequence is pretty typical. So what happens after you take the buck to the taxidermist?

First, he informs you that you may have killed a new world-record buck, and then he calls some other hunters to come over with their cameras and confirm it. They do, and within 24 hours the story is out in a local newspaper. You were never interviewed for the article.

Within a day your phone begins to ring—writers and antler buyers. They want the story and the antlers. "Will you give an exclusive? Will you sign a contract? Will you sell the antlers?"

The story appears nationally the next day. Funny thing is, you still haven't given an interview.

The telephone calls increase in frequency and insistence. "How about a television show? Will you endorse this? How about that? Can we use the buck for a sport show? Have you had it scored officially yet?"

You're overwhelmed. You sign a contract or two, taking what seems like a fair offer, a free taxidermy mount in exchange for an interview. Then you start to receive the strange calls. The first one accuses you of being a poaching publicity hound. A day later a story appears in the local paper saying you are being investigated for poaching. It's the first you've heard of it. The next day the poaching story runs nationally.

A lawyer calls. You are being sued for misrepresenting yourself in endorsing a product. You explain you never endorsed a product... as far as you know. He says you better get a lawyer.

When you hang up, your doorbell rings. It's the game warden with several policemen and reporters. The questions fly. "Did you kill your buck at night? We have affidavits from some poker players that say you arrived home with your buck around midnight."

"Not true! I mean true!" You try to explain that yes, you came home late, but you killed the buck during the day.

"Do you have witnesses?"

"Yes! No!" You explain about the two, nameless guys who helped you drag out your buck.

"Do you have pictures to corroborate your story? Did you have permission to hunt on the land?"

"It was public land," you protest.

"Can you prove it? Was your buck killed out of season? May we see the cape to confirm the buck was in its fall coat?"

You try to explain about the pile of hides. They confiscate the antlers until the matter is resolved.

That night you sit in front of your television watching the sharks feeding on your formally snow-white reputation. Your father phones to disown you. Your girlfriend calls to say it's over. Your dog won't let you touch him. You look at yourself in the mirror and wonder what you did wrong.

Now this scenario may seem far-fetched, but it isn't as exaggerated as you might believe. Ed Koberstein, well known to NAHC members as the man who harvested what was thought to be a potential new world-record whitetail in 1991, will tell you that shooting such a buck is far more trouble than it's worth.

In Ed's case, the question of poaching came up as an ugly rumor and was dutifully checked out and dismissed by local conservation officers. What's more, one of the very first stories in writing about the buck was printed without Ed's consent.

Another twist to Ed's story had to do with one of the hunters with Ed that day. It seems he took photos of Ed and his buck, but wouldn't let Ed have any of the photos to use in the many magazine articles being written about the buck. Maybe that hunter thought he could sell them for piles of money if the buck did, indeed, turn out to be a world record.

Even after countering all the allegations, Ed ended up with more problems. His buck was officially scored by experienced Boone & Crockett scorer Randy Bean. However, shortly after the buck was officially scored, Ed received a letter from B&C saying the buck would have to be rescored by a panel of scorers chaired by another official scorer of their choosing. Today the buck holds its place in the record book with a score of 188⅜—well below the world record.

Let's return to your stand that beautiful fall evening when that magnificent buck walked up. Shoot him like you did and then tag him, but this time when you walk up to him and realize he is special, forget celebrating, forget excitement, forget every natural human reaction. Think of one thing: documentation!

Somehow you absolutely have to document the event. Not only the fact it happened, but that it happened at that exact time and that exact place. For this you must have a camera, better yet a still camera and a video camera. You need a camera; if you don't have one, get one. Buy it from the farmer down the road if need be, but get a camera!

Take the camera and start snapping photos of the buck. Always have at least two rolls of film for insurance. Take a bunch of shots of the buck, including several close-ups of its face to show its eyes are not sunken. If possible, try to include something in the photos which will prove the date. Anything will help, but if you had the day's newspaper in the truck, get it and include it in the close-ups. As you leave the scene to get help, take a couple of photos from some distance away to show the location. Be sure the animal can be seen in the photo.

Go back to your truck, and this time when the vehicle with the two hunters drives up, ask them if they will take a photo of you with the buck you killed. Remember, those two hunters are your best defense against accusations of hunting illegally. They will know your buck was freshly killed, they will know where it was killed, they will know when it was killed, and they will know that circumstances dictate you were the one who killed the buck. As sad a commentary as it is, at some point you'll need to address every one of these questions.

Get them to take pictures of you with the buck, lots of pictures. There is no such thing as too many. Get them to take photos from every angle. Keep the background uncluttered. Get one of the hunters to take a couple of pictures of you and the other hunter with the buck.

The situation gets sticky if one of your helpers pulls out his own camera. The last thing you need are unauthorized stories. Suggest to the fellow that you need even more pictures and offer to buy his film. If he won't sell it to you, make sure you are in every picture he takes of the buck. Legally, he cannot publish photos of you if you have not given him permission.

After the photo session, it's time to take the buck back to your vehicle. Once you are back at your truck, get the hunters to give you their names, addresses and phone numbers. Also, get them to sign a statement of fact. Any paper, even the back of your cartridge box will do. Write down the particulars of the hunt, i.e., time, location, date and how many points you believe are on the rack. Mention that the buck was freshly killed.

When the hunters leave, they may think you are paranoid, but you'll have answers for the conservation officers when they come knocking.

By now it will be dark, but you still have to show the buck to a few more people. Drive it to the nearest farm and show the farmer. Get his name and number and get him to sign your piece of paper saying you showed up at his house at whatever time it happens to be. Remember, don't allow anyone else to take pictures.

Now take the buck directly to the nearest police station or even better to a conservation officer. Even if you have to go right to the man's house, do it. He may complain, but that'll stop when he lays eyes on your buck.

Make sure that whoever you show the buck to looks closely and notes that it has been dead for several hours. The idea is to discredit any accusations of night hunting. Have the officer check your license and tag to confirm all is in order and then, like before, get him to sign a paper saying they did so.

Until morning comes, you have done all you can. Don't do any more that night. Don't call all your friends and invite them over for a party. First thing in the morning call a photographer. You need a professional and should be prepared to pay. Unfortunately, this is also the weak link in the chain. The person who snaps the picture actually owns the copyright to the photo. In your case, it is imperative that the photographer knows you are to get the rolls of film (slide film) as they come out of the camera. Tell him that the only way you'll hire him is if he'll sign a paper stating he relinquishes copyright of the photos to you.

For these photos, the background has to be uncluttered and wilderness looking. Drive the buck to where the background is suitably wild. Skyline the antlers or have them displayed against snow. Remember, brushy backgrounds are out. Take at least 10 36-exposure rolls. Have the photographer bracket the exposures, he'll know what that means. These are the shots that will appear in the magazines later and perhaps in advertisements for products you might be asked to endorse. They have to be good.

Only after you have posed for so many pictures that your face hurts from smiling can you finally call it quits. Take your buck home and skin it out, taking care to keep the hide intact and attached to the head and antlers. Make room in your deep freeze for the cape and antlers and throw them in.

Now you can put your feet up. It's okay to take a break because it's time to go underground. If you want to tell your close friends and family, then do so, but with no interviews and no pictures.

At this point you need the advice from the powers that be. Place a call to Boone & Crockett headquarters and ask what they suggest (B&C, Dept. NAH, Old Milwaukee Depot, 250 Station Dr., Missoula, MT 59801, 406-542-1888). They'll be able to recommend an official scorer in good standing, and will arrange for you to receive a "how-to" guide about scoring. If, after receiving your B&C scoring directions and green scoring your buck, you find the antlers are going to score above the B&C minimums, you should make arrangements for an official scoring of the rack. The buck cannot be officially scored until 60 days after it was taken. You'll need the time anyway to decide what it is you want to have happen in your life for the next year.

Do you want to quit your job and do guest appearances at every outdoor show from coast to coast? Do you want your smiling face plastered beside this and that hunting product? Do you want to capitalize on your good fortune? There are those who feel the hunter who shoots the new world-record typical buck will have the opportunity to parlay his good luck into a million dollars.

Maybe, but more likely not. The "who's who" in the hunting world will be real touchy if you come across as a gold digger. Remember, it's a small fraternity and one that frowns upon the exploitation of a game animal for personal gain. Hunting is not about money and never will be.

Perhaps instead you should think about the millions of young hunters whom you'll be able to reach because of your accomplishment. We could use a hero in the hunting world. Why not you?

Regardless of what side of the fence you decide to stand on, there are three more things you should know. First, if your buck doesn't soundly beat the old world record, expect B&C officials to announce a rescore of the existing world record. Unless your buck is several inches larger than the Hanson buck, it's my prediction that you'll only be king for a day.

Second, the hot line to the NAHC headquarters is 612-936-9333.

Third, ask them to put you in touch with me.

North American Hunter Article Reference

The following articles from the *North American Hunter* archives were used in the compilation of this book. Each has been updated for timeliness and accuracy.

Article Title	Author/Issue
Do Big Bucks Really Think?	Bob Grewell May/June, 1991
Bucks By The Barometer	Robert McKinney September/October, 1992
How Deer See	Larry Weishuhn September/October, 1993
Deer On The Moon	Jeff Murray October, 1995
Dark Secrets Of Daytime Deer	Grant Wood August, 1996
Can Experts Count On Infrared?	Charles Bridwell August, 1995
Study Suggests Shooting Spikes	Larry Weishuhn September, 1995
Making Sense of Scents	Gary Clancy September, 1996

Article Title	Author/Issue
The Poop On Deer Pellets	C J. Winand October, 1996
Treeing Your Buck	Tim Jones November/December, 1996
New Wave Deer Hunting	J. Wayne Fears January/February, 1994
Feed, Scrapes, Stand (Part 1)	J. Wayne Fears July/August 1986
Feed, Scrapes, Stand (Part 2)	J. Wayne Fears September/October, 1986
Feed, Scrapes, Stand (Part 3)	J. Wayne Fears November/December, 1986
Calling All Deer (Part 1)	John Phillips July/August, 1988
Calling All Deer (Part 2)	John Phillips September/October, 1988
Calling All Deer (Part 3)	John Phillips November/December, 1988
Hunting The Nocturnal Buck	Larry Weishuhn September/October, 1994
Whitetail Feeding Frenzy	Jim Casada August, 1996
10 Steps To Better Bow Hunting	Chuck Adams August, 1995
Scrape Hunting	Ron Doss August, 1992
Trophy Hunter's Tips	John Phillips August, 1992
You Can Trail Trophy Whitetail	Jeff Murray November/December, 1991
Breaking The Ice	Judd Cooney August, 1989

Article Title	Author/Issue
Deer Calling Secrets Of The Pros	John Phillips September/October, 1991
2nd Season Whitetails	Richard P. Smith Whitetail Supplement, 1994
20 Tips For Close To Home Bucks	Jeff Murray August, 1989
Scouting The Key To Post Rut Success	Nick Sisley November/December, 1986
Early Birds Get Their Bucks	Jeff Murray January/February, 1989
Scouting After The Season In Snow Country	Greg Miller January/February, 1995
Scouting After The Season In Sun Country	Larry Weishuhn January/February, 1995
Hunting High Country Whitetails	John Haviland May/June, 1993
City's Edge Whitetails	Glenn Sapir July/August, 1994
Blue Collar Book Bucks	Glenn Sapir August, 1996
Quest For Quality Bucks	Jim Casada September Supplement, 1994
Judging Coues Deer	Chuck Adams July/August, 1989
Judging Whitetails	Chuck Adams September/October, 1989
Five Seconds For Success	Larry Weishuhn July/August, 1994
Owner's Manual To The Next World Record	Jim Shockey August, 1993